Low Pay

Low Pay

Acton Society Trust Essays
Edited by Frank Field

Arrow Books

Arrow Books Limited
3 Fitzroy Square, London W1

London Melbourne Sydney Auckland
Wellington Johannesburg Cape Town
and agencies throughout the world

First published in Arrow Books Ltd 1973
© Acton Society Trust 1973

Set in Century Schoolbook
by Lyth Engraving, Manchester
Printed in Great Britain by
Anchor Press and bound by
Wm. Brendon, both of Tiptree, Essex

ISBN 0 09 908240 3

Contents

Preface

This book arose out of a seminar the Acton Society sponsored earlier this year. Pauline Wingate and Jackie Eames of the Acton Society undertook much of the organization involved in this event. But my thanks extend beyond the Acton Society. My secretary, Jane Jessel, applied her usual skill to get the manuscript ready in time for the printers. Ruth Lister kindly commented on the three papers I was involved with, and A. B. Atkinson and Stephen Winyard were good enough to look at the section 'Social Policy and the Low Paid'. And few editors could have met with more cooperation than has been offered by Francis Bennett and his colleagues at Hutchinson in their attempts to get this book published quickly.

FRANK FIELD
June 1973

Introduction: Action on Low Pay

Frank Field
Director of the Child Poverty Action Group

In an attempt to legitimise its pay freeze, the Government has begun to express a concern for the low paid, and to declare its wish to favour them in its evolving incomes policy. This is not a new experience for those who earn least in our society. They were similarly wheeled out for exhibition when the Labour Government faced the same problem of selling its incomes policy; part of the accompanying propaganda appears to be the need to show the policy as being fair. No doubt politicians genuinely wish to help the poor in work; all that is missing is the appropriate action.

Action to help the low paid becomes difficult if, in the first place, one is not sure who the low paid are. This was apparently a question one Cabinet Minister raised during the long meeting on Stage III of the Government's incomes policy. It was, more importantly, a question which no member present at the meeting was able to answer, and Lord Rothschild's 'Think Tank' had to produce within a matter of days a paper detailing who are and who employs the low paid.

One hopes the Cabinet were shocked to learn that they are both directly, as an employer, and indirectly, through the Wages Councils, the largest employer of workers on low wages. These details are given in Nicholas Bosanquet's and Frank Field's and Stephen Winyard's essays. But more important, the essays in this book look at low pay, not as a single disadvantage for large numbers of people in this country, but as part of a wider pattern of inequality. Furthermore they aim to stimulate a debate on what can be done to raise the wages of those who earn least.

This is an urgent task. Two pieces of readily available evidence can be cited to show a recent growth in inequality. Data recently published by the Government shows that there is again a widening gap between the earnings of the lowest 10 per cent of wage earners and those on median earnings, and that there continues to be a large and persistent number of men earning less than the official poverty line. Likewise, the information on the incidence of taxation and social benefits shows that fiscal and social policies are not effective in combatting the growing inequality of rewards determined in the market place. The report (*Economic Trends* no 229, November 1972) shows that of the twelve family or household groups into which the population is divided for the Government's analysis of the incidence of taxation and social benefits, the poorest 20 per cent of eight of the groups lost ground relative to the average in 1970, while the poorest of the remaining four managed only to hold their relative position.

Evidence presented by Tony Atkinson in his papers details how low pay amongst the working population has again become one of the most important causes of poverty in post-war Britain. And the table below plots the number of families where the head of the household was in full-time work but who earned poverty wages for each of the years where information exists since 1966.

TABLE 1 *Number of working families living below the current Supplementary Benefit level*

Year	Number of Families
1966 [1]	70,000
1966 [2]	125,000
1967 [3]	62,500
1970 [4]	63,000
1972 [5]	50,000

Sources: 1) *Circumstances of Families*, HMSO, 1967 Table 2i
      2) ibid
      3) House of Commons *Hansard*, July 24 1967
      4) Two Parent Families, HMSO, 1971, p5
      5) House of Commons *Hansard*, February 5 1973

Not all the figures in the table relate to exactly the same time of year. For example, there are two sets of figures for 1966. The first relates to the earlier part of the year, and the second to when the new supplementary benefit scales came into operation. However, the data for 1970 and 1972 are comparable, for both record the numbers of the working poor at the end of the year.

If the number of families for 1970 is compared with 1972 it can be seen that there has been a drop of 13,000 in the numbers living below the poverty line. This has been largely due to the introduction of the Family Income Supplement (FIS) rather than an improvement in wage rates, but FIS is, nevertheless, a failure. Over £600,000 has been spent in an attempt to persuade the 140,000 eligible working families of the right to means-tested help. So far only half this number have claimed.

The Government, while conceding that only half of the eligible families are drawing FIS, declares that those who are entitled to the largest amounts (FIS payments can be as much as £5 a week) are already benefitting. In other words, it is only families entitled to small FIS awards who have still to claim.

While this is a defence against the low take-up of FIS it concedes that the benefit can do little now to bring the incomes of those earning low wages up to the supplementary benefit poverty line. Just how inadequate FIS is for accomplishing this task can be seen from the chapter on 'Low Pay and Social Policy'. In it details are given of families who, because of low wages when in work, are prevented from drawing their full supplementary benefit when they are dependent on social security. Those families have a notional FIS payment added to their weekly benefit, and yet, in 1971 (the latest available figures) some families were still living at over £5 below the poverty line. This figure, more than any other, shows

11

that family poverty caused by low pay must be attacked on a wider front.

A successful strategy calls for both new social policy initiatives as well as the raising of the wages of the low paid. But the dangers of attempts to help the poor by a greater dependence on means tested benefits are catalogued in Roy Moore's paper. And, furnishing further information on the ineffectiveness of present tax and social policy in creating greater equality of net incomes, he draws attention to the way our income tax system has become more regressive, and to the effects of the lowering of the tax threshold. The last point will reach its absurd conclusion if the Tax Credit proposals are introduced. Under this scheme tax of 30 per cent will be levied on the first £1 of earnings and will remain at that rate for all incomes up to £5,000.

The effect of poor families losing means-tested benefits as well as paying income tax has been described as the 'poverty trap'. The way to spring them free from it is by a combination of substantial family allowances and pay increases. All that is needed on the FA front is the will to act. But despite the effectiveness of family allowance increases in reducing the number of men and families living below the poverty line, many low wage earners express the wish to earn a fair wage for their week's work.

It is with the ways in which we can guarantee every worker a fair and proper return for his labour that this book is concerned. The papers were first presented to an Acton Society seminar. (A further one on the effects of the Equal Pay Act was, unfortunately, not completed by the time this book went to press.) The participants hope that this book will encourage and add to the growing debate on incomes policy and particularly what can be done to eliminate the unfairness of our present wage and salary structure. And they themselves hope to continue work on the strategy which is outlined in the remainder of the introduction.

In Nicholas Bosanquet's paper there is a call for the establishment of a Low Pay Board. This would not only act as a stimulus to public debate, but could very well carry out many of the proposals put forward by himself and other contributors. Its first task should be to implement the proposal which is contained in David Layton's paper. Collective bargaining has been successful in a large number of industries, both in winning substantial awards for skilled workers, and by linking the rewards of unskilled and semi-skilled to the craftsman's rates. None of these industries, such as engineering, employs a large percentage of all low paid employees, but they do contain pockets – sometimes of considerable size – of low paid workers. The Low Pay Board should set these industries the immediate target of narrowing differentials and so raise the rewards of the low paid to a higher percentage of average earnings in the industry. And from the evidence David Layton presents there is no need to expect such a policy to lead *automatically* to a re-establishment of differentials.

The second task of the Low Pay Board could be to supervise a policy for the Wages Council sector. One of the weaknesses of Wages Councils has been that none of the Councils has been given any guidance as to the wage levels they should set. It has been believed that, somehow, the rewards of Wages Council employees is a non-political question and can therefore be safely passed to the Councils who will, inevitably, make 'fair awards'. As Barbara Wootton has noted in another context, 'Decisions on issues of social policy involve judgements of value, and it is an illusion to suppose that, however "authoratative" its character, any tribunal could make such decisions impartially.' (*Social Foundation of Wages Policy,* Allen & Unwin, 1955, p.166.) Tribunal members bring prejudices and preconceived ideas to their task. So, too, do members of Wages Councils. Many members believe their task to be one of establishing subsistence level minimum rates. In this they have been all too successful. But one proposal made by Field and Winyard is for Wages Councils to be given a target wage level which all Councils would have to meet within a three year period.

This leads directly to the third function of the Low Pay Board. One of the more common concerns expressed during debates on raising the wages of the low paid is the unemployment effect of such a move. To deny the difficulties of tackling low pay, particularly in the small firm, would be unwise. Hence the need for any changes to be taken against the background of full employment, as well as for the Low Pay Board to act as a planning unit for implementing higher pay in those industries in which there are large numbers of low paid workers. In his paper, David Layton calls for work to commence, sector by sector, on the effect on negotiating higher rates of minimum pay. The Low Pay Board might also act either for or closely with the Department of Trade and Industry in channelling investment grants into low paying industries, as well as acting as consultants and technical advisers on ways in which higher wages can be matched by higher productivity.

In some parts of industry and in some areas the Low Pay Board will have to accept that higher wages for some may mean loss of employment for part of the labour force. This reinforces the point already made on the importance of conducting this policy in a situation of full employment. But the Low Pay Board should also be given the powers, as Bosanquet suggests, of coordinating and initiating retraining programmes for displaced workers.

The fourth function which could usefully be given to the Low Pay Board is to recommend policies which combat the other inequalities faced by low paid workers. A. B.

Atkinson's paper clearly demonstrates that low pay is not an accident which befalls certain people, nor is it the only disadvantage they face. Low pay and higher sickness rates go hand in hand. So too do low rewards during one's working life and poverty in old age. Social policy measures which positively favour the low paid need to be espoused by the Board.

Here, then, is the beginning of an attack on low pay. And possibly the most effective way by which the Government can show its determination to act against low pay is not only to follow the recommendations detailed in this introduction, but to also implement the two reforms called for in *Social Policy and the Low Paid*. The theme of this paper is that the needs of an economy in which a large number of workers earn low wages are imposed on our social security system. Hence the need for the four-week or workshy rules as well as the wage-stop. Could there be a more effective way open to the Government of putting pressure on those employing workers at poverty wages than to say that in future no man will lose his supplementary benefit payments until he is offered a job paying wages valued at more than his benefit? And, secondly, that no family while awaiting employment will have the wage-stop imposed against them? This is a rule which prevents a man being better off out of work than when he is filling his normal occupation. When these two reforms are conceded, we will know that the attack on low pay will have begun in earnest.

1. The Real Low Pay Problem

Nicholas Bosanquet
Labour Economist

It is easy to forget how many people are poor. The official
standard of poverty is the supplementary benefit scale
rates. Excluding the rent, which is usually paid in full,
this amounts to £1·52 a day for a married couple. At least
a fifth of the population are living in households with
incomes around this mark. (N. Bosanquet, 'Banding
Poverty', *New Society*, 1972).

About 2 million people are in households with incomes
below the mark. The numbers have shown little change
over the past decade. They are mainly the old and families.
Very few single people or childless couples before retirement are in poverty. To these in any count of the hard-
pressed have to be added people who are actually
receiving supplementary benefit. They would be in
poverty even by the restricted official definition without
it. These amount to about 4·6 million people. Most of
these are women. The elderly are also there in great
numbers. At least a further four million people have
incomes little above the supplementary benefit level.
They include 1·4 million pensioners and about 10 per
cent of families – 2·6 million people. Thus the number
of hard-pressed is about 10·6 million – 2 million below
the official poverty line, 4·6 million on it and 4 million
just above it. About 10·6 million are trying to live on 76p
a day for each married adult and 40p for each child – to
cover all out goings except rent; this estimate of numbers
is probably fairly conservative. There are no well-

demarcated frontiers to the world of the hard-pressed, no hard edges to the property band. But clearly the official map, with its sharp poverty line is a fairly misleading guide.

LITTLE IMPROVEMENT

The fortunes of many of the hard-pressed have been improving slowly if at all in recent years. This has been particularly so for poorer families in work. Even in terms of *weekly* earnings the gains were rather small. After allowing for changes in prices, taxes and national insurance contributions, the real income of a lower paid family with two children rose about 10 per cent between 1960 and 1970. (NBPI *General Problems of Low Pay* Report No. 169 HMSO CMND 4648, 1971, p 18)

This small change reflected not only general conditions such as the lack of economic growth, but particular circumstances affecting poorer families. Changes in taxes – and particularly the continued fall in the tax threshold – the level of income at which tax paying starts, bore on them rather hard. Their gain in real weekly income was in consequence less than that of more prosperous families. But even this small gain might disappear if we were able to measure directly the really crucial sum – annual income. Annual income was affected by irregularity of employment. After 1966 the labour market became what it is still – a fairly bleak place for breadwinners in poorer families. At any level of unemployment the unemployment rates of the unskilled are about 2½ times the general rate for men. (N. Bosanquet and G. Standing, 'Government and Unemployment 1966 – 70; a study of policy and evidence' *British Journal of Industrial Relations* July 1972). This means that when the unemployment rate is around 4 per cent as it was for many, many months between 1966 and 1973 the unemployment rate facing unskilled men is around 10 per cent. This is the average for the country as a whole and the position would be much worse in regions with high unemployment. Growing irregularity of employment affected many people among the hard-pressed. It affected families. But also affected pensioners. Surveys have shown that many pensioners rely on part-time work as a way of adding to their pension. Now they found such work harder to come by. The sick and the disabled also found it harder going and there were fewer new opportunities for jobs for women.

We cannot prove this directly. But it seems highly probable that the real annual household incomes of many of the hard-pressed may actually have fallen over the past few years. Developments in Sweden are further circumstantial evidence for this. The recent Report of the Low Income Commission (Ministry of the Interior Low Income Commission, *'The Structure of Incomes in Stockholm,'* Sweden, August 1970) has shown that during the 1960's some of the gains in higher earnings per hour to the lower paid were cancelled out by greater irregularity of employment even in an economy which was closer to full employment than the British one.

MULTIPLE DISADVANTAGE

Clearly people in the twilight world suffer from other disadvantages at work than those of low incomes. There are two worlds in fringe benefits and conditions of work. Occupational pensions and holidays tend to be less generous in the firms and industries which employ the hard-pressed. They have more of the inconveniences of their employment over them and they rarely have much voice through collective bargaining in questions affecting their working lives. Clearly too, they suffer from poor standards in education, health and housing. A better chance for the hard-pressed needs changes in the pattern

19

of taxation and in the social services. For most pensioners the really important question will continue to be the level of pensions. For families it is inconceivable that pay can be related precisely to circumstances – hence the need for a generous level of family allowances. If we are to end the division between worlds we need changes in the way work is regulated, in the social services, in pensions and in family allowances. But such changes are not a substitute for a policy of raising the relative earnings of the low paid. If we are serious about ending the division between worlds, we need both changes in social policy, *and* a policy for low pay. Without such a policy it will be difficult to raise social security benefits to a more reasonable level. These are bound to be affected by the level of low pay. Low pay in work affects peoples private and public pension entitlements. Without a policy for low pay people will continue to feel demeanded and shamed by the pitifully small amounts that they earn at work.

Not everybody who is low paid is hard-pressed. The second pay packet of a working wife may bring affluence to a family: a couple in their fifties may live in comfort on a wage which seems very low. Thus it has to be accepted that action on the behalf of the low paid will benefit numbers of people whose circumstances are comfortable. But there is no way of helping the hard-pressed which does not involve this spreading of benefits. The iniquities of inaction are greater than those of action.

DEFINING LOW PAY

A policy for low pay needs a definition. The NBPI in its report *General Problems of Low Pay,* (Report No. 169 HMSO London CMND 4648, 1971) defined low pay in terms of the lowest decile – the worst paid ten per cent in the labour force. It took separate deciles for men and women workers. But in terms of hourly earnings this would mean taking as the mark of low pay about 30p an hour for women workers. In this paper, the low paid are defined in terms of an arbitrary standard of hourly earnings – of 50p an hour for men and 35p an hour for women in April 1972. 9·5 per cent of full time male workers over twenty-one and 16·3 per cent of full time women workers over ·18 had earnings below these marks in April 1972. The phrase 'low pay' is sometimes used about several difficult situations. Sometimes it points to a level of pay which is low in absolute terms: but it can also refer to pay which is low in relation to skill, responsibility or the onerousness of the job. Here we are talking mainly about low pay in the literal sense.

A policy for low pay also needs a clear aim. Public discussion has often been carried out about a false choice – between doing nothing and introducing a minimum level of earnings of £20–£25 a week for all workers overnight. The real choice is between inaction and action which might over a period of five years mean progress towards limited and carefully defined objectives. These objectives might be to raise the hourly earnings of women from about 55 to about 75 per cent of men hourly earning and of ensuring that (in current terms) no adult male worker was getting less than £22·50 for a 40 hour week. How realistic is such a policy? Would it have undesirable effects on the employment of the lower paid? It has been argued from international evidence that such a policy for low pay might increase teenage unemployment, enforce retirements, hamper regional policy and increase the employment difficulties of the disabled. Anxiety about the employment effects of policies for low pay caused severe paralysis of the will under the last Labour Government. The prize of a successful policy – ending the gulf between the worlds – is a great one. But is the price too high?

Much of this debate has been carried out in terms of evidence from the past in Britain and from other countries. We turn now to this evidence, and to three questions:

What were the circumstances which surrounded past policies for low pay in Britain?

What is the pattern of low pay today? How does it differ from the pattern in the past?

What does the international evidence show about the effects of various policies for low pay?

PREVIOUS POLICIES

The question of low pay came to light as our society's wealth grew. In a labour surplus economy with a low-level of real income, the important question is not that of the low pay of a minority – even a substantial one – but that of the poverty or even destitution of a majority. In Britain the question of low pay first came into general discussion in the 1880s. The focus was on conditions in sweated trades such as tailoring. Forces both on the demand and on the supply side had depressed wages in these trades. On the demand side activities such as the workshop-based London tailoring industry was facing intense competition from provincial factories. On the supply side the weakest groups in a labour surplus economy – women and very young workers – had to take what they could get. The effects of unbridled competition was to depress wages far below the minimum needed for physical subsistence. The typical low paid worker between 1880 and 1914 worked in a small shop in a handi-craft industry which was declining in face of competition from factory methods of production. In this kind of market, with producers and workers both facing desperate competition from their fellows, there were few limits to degradation.

During the 1880s there was a good deal of debate about the causes of sweating. The view of Beatrice Webb came to hold the field. She attributed sweating partly to the spirit of unrestrained competition and also to lack of union organisation and state regulation. She wrote how the 'contrast between the sweated workers of East London and the Lancashire textile operatives made me realize how the very concentration of wage-earners ... had made possible ... collective regulation of the conditions of employment which in the Factory Acts and mines regulations on the one hand and in the standard rate of wages and the working day of Trade Unions had during the latter part of the nineteenth century wrought so great an improvement in the regulated section of the world of labour.' (B. Webb, *My Apprenticeship*, Penguin 1971, p 347.)

When after many years of desultory discussion the Liberal Government finally carried through the Trade Boards Act, it reflected among other sources of inspiration the philosophy of Beatrice Webb. The Trade Boards were designed both to raise wages of sweated workers and to provide the nearest possible approximation to free collective bargaining, and their lack of success is detailed in the following paper. This philosophy again underpinned the rapid extension of Trade Boards immediately after the First World War, but suffered a severe setback as a result of the Report of the Cave Committee which recommended that Trade Boards should concern themselves only with minimum standards of subsistence. But the principle of making Trade Boards (renamed Wages Councils) as similar as possible in their method of operation to free collective bargaining was once again central to the Wages Council Act of 1945.

Today it is hardly possible to believe that the extension of collective bargaining could take place very quickly – or even if it did not that it would make very much difference to pay. Some low paid workers – particularly in the public sector are already quite strongly organised and union membership has not prevented Co-op workers from being among the lowest paid of shop workers. How analogous, too, is the old pattern of low pay to the pattern today? Are the industrial origins of low pay the same as in the past – or have an entirely new set of circumstances grown up since the war?

WHO ARE THE LOW PAID?

Where do low paid men – those earning less than 50p an hour work? We can start by looking for a rather distinct group – the very low paid. They earn less than 40p an hour. Nearly half of these work in the hotel and catering trades. The rest are in service activities such as garages and in agriculture. Turning to the low paid, we again find that they are highly concentrated in the services and in agriculture. Again workers in hotels are particularly likely to be low paid. But we also find many low paid workers in shops. Low paid men are not scattered around fairly evenly between industries. They are highly concentrated in the services. Nor can low earnings in the services be attributed to tips and payments in kind. Surveys have shown these to be small. Even in hotels we hear a great deal about the rich pickings that may go to the waiter – but rather less about the fact that the porter may well get nothing.

The low paid are not concentrated in any particular region. In some regions – such as the South West and East Anglia – high proportions of all workers were low paid: other regions had low proportions but large numbers. 23·7 per cent of low paid male workers are in the South East. The most important concentration is in terms of age. About 40 per cent of the low paid are over fifty. There is some tendency for disabled workers to be low paid. But the great majority of low paid men are not special cases.

Like low paid men, low paid women are concentrated in the services, although to a slightly lesser extent. Women white collar workers figure significantly among the low paid – unlike their male colleagues. In general both for men and for women low pay is related to a broad split between the services and agriculture and manufacturing in levels of pay. A similar divide is to be found in the United States, France and Sweden as well as in Great Britain. In all four countries two thirds of the low paid work outside manufacturing – in the services and in agriculture. Clearly the pattern today in Britain is rather different from that of the past. Before the First World War, the typical low paid worker was employed in a declining handcraft industry. Now the typical low paid worker is a porter in a hotel, a shop assistant or a farm worker. Low pay used to be related to declining employment in an industry and to low levels of profit-ability. These associations are still found – as with laundries – but they are not generally the case. Hotels and agriculture are examples of fairly profitable activities, which in the case of hotels have been expanding their employment but which pay very little.

CAUSES OF LOW PAY

The evidence on the causes of low pay also tends to show the importance of industry as compared to occupation and to personal characteristics. It is sometimes argued that low pay reflects low personal productivity. The low paid are not worth more. However the evidence suggests that many factors other than personal handicap are important. One way of testing the relative weight of the occupational and the industrial factors is to look at the earnings of a particular grade of worker across all industries. If the occupational factor was very important we would expect the pay levels of the unskilled to be very similar across all industries. But in fact the evidence suggests that the pay levels of the unskilled are closely related to the average pay levels of the industries in which they work. The unskilled tend to have high earnings in manufacturing and low earnings in the services. Recent research in the United States has also shown the importance of the industry effect. Wachtel and Betsy (H. M. Wachtel and C. Betsy, 'Employment at Low Wages', *Review of Economics and Statistics, 1972),* have shown that people working as labourers with the same personal characteristics – education, years on the job, race etc. – earned from $4708 to $6136 depending on the industry in which they worked.

Does international experience provide a strong argument against a policy for low pay? It is sometimes said that the effects of the minimum wage system in America have been unfortunate. Until recently the balance of evidence suggested that the minimum wage had had substantial effects on employment. An early study by Douty (H. Douty, 'Some effects of the Minimum Wage in the US', *Economical,* May 1965) looked at the effects of the 1965 increase from 75c to $1 an hour. The study looked at twelve industries mainly in the South which had been particularly affected. It showed some sharp increases in wage levels, For example in Southern saw milling, straight time hourly earnings rose about 17·6 per cent. In the year following the wage increase there were employment declines in all but two of the industries studied – ranging from 3·2 per cent to 15 per cent. Other studies suggested that the minimum wage had led to differential faster increases in teenage unemployment and in black unemployment; had reduced the growth rate of employment in rural countries in Florida; and had led to the substitution of capital for labour in low wage industries.

But more recent studies have begun to show a rather different set of conclusions. Early studies had looked at the effects of the minimum wage as if this was the only factor at work in the labour market. But discussion of teenage employment has to be seen against a background of rapid growth in the teenage labour force. While the total population over 16 grew by 19·4 per cent between 1954 and 1967, the teenage population rose by over 60 per cent. One recent study has looked at the rate of job creation – at employment rather than unemployment. It showed that in fact the rate of job creation for teenagers was much faster than for the population as a whole. (P. S. Barth, 'The Minimum Wage and Teenage Employment', *I.R.R.A. Proceedings*, 1969). The statistical evidence suggests that the rate was not much affected by changes in the minimum wage. But perhaps the most important new study is that of the U.S. Department of Labour *Youth Unemployment and Minimum Wages*. (U.S. Government Printing Office, Washington, 1970). This is much more comprehensive and statistically careful study than has been carried out before. It shows that changes in the teenage population, in the rate of draft calls and in school enrolment were a much more important influence on teenage employment than changes in the minimum wage. At the very least the new studies show the rashnesss of dogmatic conclusions about the American experience.

SWEDISH EXPERIENCE

The other experience abroad which may be relevant – although in a different economy and society is that of Sweden. In Sweden the main way of helping the low paid has been through collective bargaining rather than through minimum wage legislation. The official objective of the 'solidary' wage policy has been to create just and reasonable relationships between the various groups of wage earners. In practice this has led to attempts to narrow differentials in favour of the lower paid. Policy has concentrated on three types of differential – those between the sexes, between industries and between persons within industries. The evidence suggests that the policy has been fairly successful in narrowing all these differentials. Most success has been achieved in narrowing the differential between persons and between industries. Taking the broadest average of hourly earnings, in the late 1950s women's earnings were 70 per cent of men's; at the beginning of the 1970s they were 83 per cent. Among industries the spread narrowed – both the very high paid and the very low paid moved nearer to the average. The effect was greatest for the highest paid. The two highest paid industries – construction and mining went down from 145·4 per cent and 124·6 per cent of the manufacturing industry average in 1964 to 130·9 per cent and 119·7 per cent in 1970. There was also some narrowing of differentials within industries. In addition certain occupations particularly low paid workers in hospitals and government service – received specially large increases. All this came about – in association with an active policy of manpower retraining – without serious employment effects. (N. Bosanquet, *Low Pay: an International Comparison of Patterns and Policies*, OECD, forthcoming).

What does the balance of evidence suggest about the economic constraints on a policy for low pay? Would such a policy lead to an unacceptably large loss of jobs, and to the exclusion of weaker workers from the labour force? When the subject first came under serious study in Britain it seemed that there might be rather bad effects. A pioneering study by Judith Marquand emphasized a strong relationship between low pay and contractions in employment. (J. Marquand, 'Which are the lower paid workers?' *British Journal of Industrial Relations*, November 1967). But her study was limited to manufacturing, in which a minority of the low paid work. Another study has brought to light the division between the services and manufacturing and the associations between low pay and expanding employment. (N. Bosanquet and R. J. Stephens, 'Another Look at Low Pay *Journal of Social Policy,* July 1972).

The more worrying association is between low pay and age. However policies for full employment and for retraining – accompanying one for low pay – would do much to mitigate unfavourable consequences for older workers. In essence a full employment economy, in which many of the low paid are working in expanding industries, provides a rather novel setting for a policy for low pay. Unaccompanied by full employment and policies for retraining, a policy for low pay could be dangerous. But accompanied by such policies the benefits to many individuals could be rather great. Nor does the international experience give serious grounds for pessimism.

WIDENING GAP

The alternative to a policy for low pay is a growing inequality in incomes. This will arise in part from change in the labour market. The proportion of professional and managerial workers in the labour force is growing year by year. Many of these are young – reflecting recent expansions in higher education. This new generation is taking and will, other things being equal, continue to take in the future a growing share in national income. Change in the labour market will help to produce a growing inequality in reward between older and younger generations. This may seem particularly inequitable because higher education is financed from the taxes paid by the older generation. In so far as training and education are still more open to men than to women, change in the labour market will also lead to greater inequality between men and women. But growing inequality of incomes could also result from the impact of certain strongly held attitudes about pay. In practice the greatest gulf in pay and living standards is between the top 10 per cent of male salaried workers and the rest of the labour force. At the start of his working life the young professional earns more than most manual workers at the peak of their lifetime earnings: his earnings go on rising steeply well into his working life. But it is generally *believed* that the greatest gulf in pay is between the 'affluent worker' – car-workers and dock workers – and the rest of the community. In fact the earnings of manual workers are often much exaggerated. About eighty per cent of adult male manual workers were earning less than £40 a week in April 1972 and 98 per cent were earning less than £60 a week. But the common view is rather different. Without a policy for low pay we are likely to see an increasingly bitter struggle for income shares between manual workers and salaried workers, in which the advantage is likely to be to the latter. The result is likely to be a growing inequality and increasing strife. Given these tensions no incomes policy is likely to be durable which does not have a redistributive element. To succeed it has to mean equality in restraint between professional and manual workers. Considerations of political prudence point here in the same direction as those of equity.

What form could a policy for low pay take? The two main alternatives are a national minimum wage and redistribution through a national incomes policy. The past history of British policy as well as of policy abroad would tend to suggest that the national minimum wage is something of a blind alley. Britain has had for many years a minimum wage system of a peculiar kind. This is the Wages Council system. However, as Field and Winyard show, the Wages Councils are not having much positive effect on levels of pay. They have certainly not led to any increase in the relative earnings of their clients.

They may even have acted to reduce the rate of increase in pay, in face of labour shortages in the hotel trade and elsewhere. Nor have they done much either to stimulate the growth of collective bargaining or to provide an effective substitute for it. They have concerned themselves with a limited range of subjects: with rates rather than with earnings: with holidays rather than with the whole range of fringe benefits. They have done little to secure occupational pensions for their clients. Normally under full employment and collective bargaining, the inconveniences of an employment arising from fluctuations in workload or from other causes, should be fairly shared. But in some Wages Council industries the inconveniences of employment fall almost entirely on the worker. In hotels staff work split shifts, weekends and evenings for very little extra reward. Nor is there joint regulation of how tips are distributed.

In general the Wages Councils have not been effective guardians of the lower paid. There were two main reasons for this failure. First, too much responsibility was on Governments and on the independent members of the Councils. They were being asked to take rather fundamental decisions of politics – about raising the earnings of the lower paid relatively faster without proper guidance from the Government, and in their paper Field and Winyard suggest that such guidance should now be given in the form of wage targets. Secondly, the Wages Councils are too close to the circumstances of individual industries. They have given more weight to the possible difficulties of employers than to the injustices to workers implied by very low rates of pay. This second difficulty would not apply to a national minimum wage policy. But the first emphatically would. Such a policy would, to be successful involve bold action by Government, action for which over many years Governments have shown themselves to be incapable.

International evidence from France and the United States also shows the limited effects of minimum wage policies. The legislation has done little to improve the relative position of the lower paid in those countries. Minimum wage laws are a fairly primitive way of giving some protection to the lower paid in countries with weak collective bargaining.

Recent history in Britain shows another false trail. Official thinking has been much concerned with raising efficiency in low paid industries. Thus the Fourth Report of the NBPI said in 1969,

'In so far as improving the position of the low paid is one of the purposes of a prices and incomes policy – which in our view it should be – the main remedy is to be found in the improvement of efficiency'.

This theme figured strongly in a number of the Board's Reports – particularly those on the clothing industry and on local authority manual workers. Even the TUC has put great weight on improving efficiency. Both Government and unions have adopted at times the David Copperfield approach to low pay. Certainly there is some scope for raising efficiency of the low paid. A study by Brynley Thomas et al, of a small firm in the Yorkshire clothing industry, has shown how training effectively raised the earnings of low paid women workers. *(British Journal of Industrial Relations* July 1969). But the efficiency of the high paid and even of the professional and academic classes could no doubt do with some improvement as well. Fundamentally the question of low pay is one of equity – not of efficiency.

INCOMES POLICY

The alternative approach to a minimum wage distribution through a national incomes policy – starts with the great strength of a favourable public opinion behind it. But such a policy must take account of other pre-occupations, which unless given due attention may in the longer-term destroy its acceptability. Two separate problems have often been confused under the heading 'low pay'. One is that of low pay in the literal sense. The other is that of pay which is low in relation to skill and responsibility. Policy so far has dealt with low pay in the literal sense and has done little for the rest. But there is a great deal of suppressed resentment here.

A second pre-occupation is the sense of unfairness felt by workers in the public sector. In a number of major industrial countries – France and the United States – as well as Britain, there have been disputes in recent years about the pay of public employees. But the conflict has been most acute in Britain. This was even so in the 1950s with difficulties over railway pay, and in the early 1960s with the pay of nurses and probation officers. But it was from 1969 on that resentment became really strong. Workers in the public sector felt that they had been treated unfairly by the Labour Government's incomes policy. This resentment helped to bring about the wage explosion and was evidenced in long strikes by dustmen, postmen and miners. By the middle of 1972, this fire of resentment may have burnt low. But the ashes are still glowing.

Just as the attitudes and feelings of workers in the public sector are distinctive, so is the economic setting in which they work. National agreements are generally more important in the public sector. There are few opportunities for shop-floor bargaining. Part of the private sector trades internationally and generally enterprises operate in a commercial context. The economic limits to wage bargaining are tighter in the private sector. Pay in the public sector cannot be set without taking into account questions of equity.

As well as dealing with low pay in the literal sense, policy must also help people whose pay is low in relation to skill and responsibility and establish equity as between public and private employees. Policy must also deal with worries about the effects on employment and on rickety firms of a faster relative increase in the earnings of the low paid. This will require, as well as high levels of employment generally special help for workers and for firms.

The first part of any policy is a national agreement between unions, employers and government on the pace of pay advance. This general agreement would be translated into detail through a document such as the Pay Code and would be administered by a body such as the Pay Board. Stage two of the current policy has certainly seen a start towards redistribution. It has meant that increases of 10 per cent or more to the low paid and 4 per cent or less to people on salaries of more than £5,000, although, of course, in money terms the gap between workers on low and high earnings is still widening. The exact amount of redistribution will have to be decided through bargaining year by year. But we should probably aim at another couple of years with at least as much redistribution as has taken place through stage two of the current policy. However, such redistribution will be achieved more easily with some modifications of approach.

The present policy affects some redistribution within groups. It sets out guidelines for collective bargaining within normal bargaining groups. But often this may mean redistribution from the badly paid to the very badly paid. Low paid industries and occupations tend to have one set of bargaining groups, highly paid industries and occupations another set. Nor does this approach help to get a balance between the claims of the private sector and those of the public sector. The aim should be to widen out bargaining groups so that the claims of the low paid and of the high paid can be looked at together. In some cases there are natural frontiers for a wider bargaining group. The NHS could be looked at as a whole. In practice the best way to get such wider groupings may be to look at the pace of pay advance as between broad sectors – manufacturing, private services, public services, the nationalized industries and construction. Through discussion, a pattern of rates of increase might be agreed between sectors. But as under the existing code this would have to leave some freedom for bargainers at the industry level. Such a policy would allow some consideration both of the claims of the absolutely low paid – the majority of whom work in private service industries – and of people who are low paid in relation to skill and responsibility. Most of the latter work in the public sector.

The problems of some groups in the public sector are too pressing to be dealt with on such a general basis. Public sympathy has quite presciently identified certain groups, who are rather badly treated at present. These are nursing, remedial and technical and ancillary staff in the NHS. A new policy should aim to set fairer pay structures and pay levels for these groups.

The main need is for fairer rewards for training. For example in nursing, untrained nursing auxiliaries are in fact relatively well paid. But after stoppages, the pay of a single student nurse is currently 22p. an hour, of a staff nurse 42p. and of a ward sister 52p. The rewards for trained physiotherapists, radiographers and speech therapists are also pitifully small. Among catering grades the worst inequities may be in the pay of skilled and supervisory staff rather than in that of unskilled workers. Already with the recent fall in unemployment, hospitals are finding recruitment more and more difficult. Assuming that we remain nearer to full employment than was the case between 1970 and 1972, staffing difficulties are likely to get much worse over the next few years.

The National Board for Prices and Incomes showed what could be done in its Reports on Armed Forces Pay and on the Pay of the Industrial Civil Service. The NBPI recommended a new pay structure and substantial increase in pay levels for the Armed Forces. Clearly the work of the armed forces is very different from that of staff in the NHS. But some of the problems of setting pay are rather similar. One question in the Armed Forces was that of differentials between grades and of setting pay roughly in line with jobs of comparable responsibility in outside industry.

Another problem was that of producing a more unified salary structure – rationalizing the pattern of allowances. A third question was that of the weight to be attached to the special conditions of service work. The NBPI carried out a large exercise in job evaluation – a special technique of comparing the content of various jobs. It succeeded in doing this not only for jobs such as those of fitter which has close analogues outside but for those of officers which did not have close analogues. Similar exercises should be carried out for groups in the NHS.

In its Report on the *Industrial Civil Service,* the NBPI suggested a new pay structure. One question here was the very low wage of skilled men, particularly in the dockyards. In the last three years, on the basis of this Report great improvements have been made in the pay of industrial civil servants.

Measures to help staffs in the NHS would not only have the strong support of public opinion and give cogency to policy. They would help to deal with a most serious recruitment crisis. Without such action it will be difficult to recruit remedial staff, and nursing staff: and our hospitals will soon be desperately short of clerical and service staff.

LOW PAY BOARD

To deal with anxieties about the future of vulnerable workers and firms we need a Low Pay Board. The main obstacle to an effective policy for low pay in Britain has been doubts about its effects on some contracting industries. This would have duties both towards firms and towards workers in low paid industries. To firms, it would have the power and staff to give technical and consultancy advice. It would be able to give investment grants and in certain circumstances to pay compensation to firms in the event of closures.

For workers the Low Pay Board would coordinate the training activities of government in so far as they affected the low paid. It would have a watching brief and a right to be consulted. For example it would try to ensure that workers in low paid industries and firms were getting benefit from the expansion of Government Training Centres. It would also work to improve the opportunities of less well qualified school-leavers. At present thousands of young people are leaving schools, without a good standard of education and are going into dead-end jobs. Training has until now been concentrated on better qualified school leavers and at craft level and above. The educational Reports of the 1960s touched only sketchily on the employment problems of the 'Newsom' child. A Low Pay Board would have to do a good deal of work on the facts: it could then insist on an expansion of opportunities. The ranks of the low paid are replenished every generation.

We also need a reform of the Wages Council system. It should be concerned less with pay – which will be mainly under the rubric of the Pay Board or its successor bodies – than with giving effective protection to the lower paid on conditions of work and fringe benefits. The basic need is for new legislation – both to make it easier to extend

37

collective bargaining and to provide more effective protection to workers who are not likely to be covered by collective bargaining in the near future. The rationale and methods of state intervention need the basic rethinking which they have not received since 1909. The initial move here might have to be a Royal Commission or Departmental committee.

Worked at over a period of years, these policies would do much, in conjunction with the right policies for taxation for pensions and for family allowances to bring the hard-pressed into the wider society. The main danger is that our society will become increasingly divided between the affluent and the less well off. On one side will be the world of youth and opportunities – on the other the poor. We have already constructed one unpleasant private world for the old. A policy for low pay could do much to avert further division.

2. Low Pay in Public Employment and the Wages Council Sector

Frank Field
Director of the Child
Poverty Action Group

Stephen Winyard
Research Officer, London
Borough of Kingston

This paper looks at the extent to which the Government is responsible both directly, as an employer, and indirectly, through the Wages Council sector, for the employment of a very large number of workers on poverty wages. The first section examines the industrial distribution of low paid workers. This is followed by a short analysis of low pay in the public sector. The main body of the paper looks at a less well-known area of Government responsibility, namely the Wages Council sector. The conclusion is devoted to a number of policy recommendations.

WHO EMPLOYS THE LOW PAID?

Table 2.1 ranks the main industrial groupings according to the percentage of all male low paid workers employed within each major industry. £22 a week was chosen as the cut-off point for low paid male workers in full-time employment. This is the level in the 1972 *NES* nearest to the current TUC demand for giving priority to workers earning less than £22.50. We have taken a proportionately higher figure of low pay for the cut-off point for female workers and set this at 70 per cent of average female weekly earnings. Table 2.2 details the results of this analysis.

The two industries which account for a third of all low paid men are Distributive and Miscellaneous services, and both include a large number of Wages Councils. For example, hotels and catering, laundries and hairdressing are grouped together with other smaller industries into Miscellaneous Services. The fourth largest employer of the low paid is central and local government. These three sectors alone account for over four out of ten low paid male workers. If agriculture is added – which has a Wages Board – then one has located almost half of all men in low paid employment.

The same analysis has been carried out for female employment. In this case, over half of all low paid female workers are employed in Distribution and Miscellaneous Services. As with male employment, the Distribution Grouping covers eleven of the fifty-one wages councils.

It is also of interest to look at the percentage of workers in each industry that are low paid. This information is readily available in the Department of Employment's New Earnings Survey and shows, for example, that although agriculture accounts for only seven per cent of all low paid men nationally, over 40 per cent of agricultural workers are low paid. In the cases of women workers, the clothing industry which is covered by ten Wages Councils, whilst accounting for six per cent of all low paid women nationally has nearly one-third of its female workforce earning less than £14 per week. It is evident that an industry may be responsible for only a small part of the national problem yet workers within it can have a high probability of being low paid.

This analysis has not, however, been presented to challenge the widely accepted view that low paid workers are to be found in all industries. The tables show this to be true. Its aim is to concentrate attention on those industries employing most of the low paid and to highlight which bodies are responsible for determining the rewards of these workers.

TABLE 2.1 *Percentage of all low paid men nationally, manual and non-manual, employed in each industry (earning less than £22) – April 1972*

Distributive Trades	17.1
Miscellaneous Services	15.3
Construction	9.0
Public Administration	8.4
Professional and Scientific Services	8.3
Agriculture	7.0
Transport and Communications	4.9
Mechanical Engineering	4.2
Insurance and Banking	3.1
Textiles	2.8
Food and Drink	2.5
Other Metal Goods	2.4
Electrical Engineering	2.0
Timber	1.7
Metal Manufacture	1.6
Clothing	1.5
Paper and Printing	1.4
Vehicles	1.1
Other Manufacturing	1.1
Chemicals	0.9
Bricks etc	0.8
Gas, Electricity and Water	0.8
Ship Building	0.7
Instrument Engineering	0.5
Leather Goods etc	0.4
Mining	0.4
Coal and Petrol Products	0.1

THE PUBLIC SECTOR

Nearly one and a half million workers are employed in Public Administration and it is not a new experience for many of them to be low paid. In 1886 roadworkers, pavement and sewage workers ranked seventh from the bottom of thirty-eight industrial groupings. By 1906 they were the worst paid of all fifty-eight groupings. During the inter-war depression years, their position improved. By 1924 they were fifth from the bottom of forty-one ranked

TABLE 2.2   *Percentage of all low paid women nationally, manual and non-manual, employed in each industry (earning less than £14) – April 1972*

Distribution	31.3
Miscellaneous Services	21.3
Professional and Scientific	12.5
Clothing	5.7
Textiles	4.0
Insurance and Banking	3.9
Food, Drink and Tobacco	3.4
Other Metal Goods	2.2
Paper, Printing etc	1.9
Agriculture	1.9
Electrical Engineering	1.7
Other Manufacturing	1.5
Mechanical Engineering	1.5
Transport and Communications	1.4
Public Administration	1.3
Construction	0.9
Chemicals	0.8
Timber, Furniture etc	0.7
Bricks, Pottery etc	0.6
Metal Manufacture	0.6
Instrument Engineering	0.4
Vehicles	0.4
Gas, Electricity and Water	0.1
	100.%

Source for Tables 2.1 and 2.2: Doe Gazette, December 1972 and Annual Employment Statistics

industries; in 1928 they were seventh worst paid and in 1931 fifteenth from the bottom. The cause of this relative improvement was that wages of workers in the public sector remained static while those all about them experienced wage cuts. As soon as the depression gave way to an improved industrial performance, public utility workers again experienced a fall in their relative living standards. By 1938 they ranked fourth lowest out of seventeen industrial groupings. At the end of the war workers in the public services again occupied the bottom position in the earnings league table. Lowest again in 1948, they remained there until 1971, the latest available data in this series. They had the lowest average weekly earnings of the twenty-four industrial groups analysed in October 1971. *(Department of Employment Gazette,* Table 122, December 1972). It is worth remembering that the welfare state services, which account for a large number of workers in the public sector, have not only been financed by taxpayers. The workers in this sector have subsidized, and continue to contribute a considerable subsidy in the form of drawing low wages. Little wonder, then, the Secretary of State for Social Services refuses to publish a list of those bodies employing workers drawing the new poverty benefit, the Family Income Supplement.

WAGES COUNCILS

A second area where workers have continuously fared badly is the Wages Council sector. Here the Government has indirect responsibility for the levels of minimum reward in each Wages Council. Wages Councils (originally known as Boards) were first established in 1909. The aim was to abolish the poverty wages associated with the sweated trades. By establishing Wages Councils, as they became known in 1945, the Government accepted the responsibility for the minimum rewards in these industries. Our contention is that they have never attempted to influence Wages Councils to improve radically the relative position of Wages Council employees. The only times influence has been brought to bear on Wages Councils has been during an incomes freeze when the aim was to prevent wage increases. This happened in 1948, 1952, 1958, 1961 and again at the end of the sixties.

Today something like three and a half million workers are covered by Wages Councils. They include six large areas of employment – retail distribution, hotel and catering, the clothing industries, hairdressing, laundries and road haulage. Agriculture is also covered by two Wages Boards.

The Councils brought two new principles into industrial relations. The first was to set a legal minimum wage for workers in each establishment. The second was the power of enforcement given to Wages Council Inspectors. Councils are composed of three parts, consisting of representatives from both sides of industry, together with three independent members. The following two sections of this paper examine how effective Wages Councils have been in eliminating the sweating and excesses of low pay. It also reviews the effectiveness of the enforcement procedure. Writing in the early sixties Guillebaud concluded: 'There are many good grounds for affirming that the machinery of the Wages Council system has achieved the general purpose for which it was established. It has virtually abolished the evils of sweated labour and the competitive under-cutting of wages. It has raised morale and with it the efficiency of the labour employed in the industries concerned *and has diminished in a marked degree the more extreme inequalities in wages between different industries and within the same industry'.*(Our italics) (see C. W. Guillebaud, *The Wages Council System in Great Britain,* Nisbet, 1962.)

Do these sweeping conclusions stand up to a detailed examination?

Immediately we are faced with a major problem, namely the lack of adequate comparative data. The records are very incomplete and especially for the early years, but the following paragraphs attempt to piece together what is known about Wages Council rates of pay at the turn of the century up until the present day.

Tables 2.3 and 2.4 summarize much of the known data.
Table 2.3 has selected what were to become Wages
Council industries from the league table of the fifty-eight
major industrial groups ranked in 1906 according to the
level of average payments. The same information is

TABLE 2.3   *Selected low paying industries in 1906.*
Fifty-eight industries ranked according to average
weekly earnings.

Industry	Ranking
Jute	57
Linen etc.	56
Aerated Water	52
Flax and Hemp	51
Laundry	49
Baking	35
Shirtmaking	29
Sugar Confectionery	21
Ready Made Tailoring	17

TABLE 2.4   *Selected low pay industries for the inter-*
War Years. Forty-one industries ranked according
to average weekly earnings

	1924	1928	1931	41 = lowest industry
	Ranking by average weekly earnings			
Linen	41	41	41	
Laundry	39	40	38	
Cutlery	38	38	40	
Baking	30	32	33	
Sugar Confectionery	5	8	6	

Source for tables 2.3 and 2.4: *British Labour Statistics,* Historical
Abstract, HMSO, 1971.

presented in Table 2.4 for the three inter-war years for which the information is available. From the two tables it can be seen that linen, laundry and baking continue to appear both as low paying industries in 1906 and throughout the period following World War I.

The first comprehensive data for the post-war world were collected in 1960. These were analysed by Judith Marquand in a study entitled 'Which are the Low Paid Workers?' (*British Journal of Industrial Relations,* November 1967). In doing so, she highlighted structural characteristics which were associated with low pay. They were:

(1) A high proportion of women workers;

(2) A high proportion of unskilled workers;

(3) Industries dominated by small firms;

(4) Contracting industries;

(5) Particular institutional factors such as Wages Councils or government employment.

Although Marquand made special reference to Wages Councils, the first four structural characteristics also apply to them. For example, nearly two-thirds of all workers in the Wages Council sector are women. Not surprising, then, were her findings on ranking industries according to earnings at the lowest decile and lowest quartile. Of those twenty industries where the lowest paid workers were relatively low paid, sixteen were covered by Wages Council industries or public administration. And she concluded:

'It is possible that Wages Councils, while perhaps ensuring that earnings in their industries are higher than they would otherwise have been, still make awards which lead to relatively low earnings in their industries.'

This finding is borne out by two additional sets of information which bring up to date the earnings figures. The following tables look at those Wages Councils detailed in the NES for 1968, 1970 and 1972. They measure for both men and women the difference between the lowest decile in Wages Council industries and average earnings in all industries. Without exception the gap between the rewards of the lowest paid 10 per cent of Wages Council employees and average wages widened for each group during the periods under study.

TABLE 2.5 *Male manual workers*
Difference between lowest decile in wages council industry and average earnings in all industries

Wages Council industry	1968 £	1970 £	1972 £
Licensed Residential Establishments	14.4	15.4	18.5
Agriculture	10.8	11.9	14.2
Retail Drapery	10.3	10.4	13.8
Milk Distributive	5.9	5.3	6.7
Road Haulage	5.3	6.3	7.0

TABLE 2.6 *Female manual workers*
Difference between lowest decile in Wages Council industry and average earnings in all industries

Wages Council industry	1968 £	1970 £	1972 £
Licensed Residential Establishments	4.8	5.8	7.5
Retail Food Trades (E & W)	4.0	4.6	6.0
Industrial and Staff Canteens	3.8	4.9	6.6
Retail Furnishing	3.6	4.1	5.8
Retail Drapery	3.5	3.6	5.2
Dressmaking	2.8	4.1	5.4
Readymade and Wholesale Bespoke Tailory	2.6	3.4	4.4

Source for Tables 2.5 and 2.6: *NES* 1968, 1970 and 1972.

The second set of information comes from Incomes Data Services Ltd. In their September 1970 report they made a comparison between pay increases and price increases for the low-paid. Just as their August report had concluded that:

'There can be no doubt from our evidence that Wages Council industries, as a group, are by far the worst off and that of the thirty-two groups in the lowest quarter, twenty-four were Wages Council industries,'

so this report spotlighted the deteriorating purchasing power for workers in Wages Council industries. In the five years up to the report's publication, retail prices rose by 24.7 per cent. During this period, in twenty-five out of fifty-three Wages Councils the lowest minimum rates of pay for men rose by less than 24.7 per cent. From September 1968 to September 1970 prices rose by 12.1 per cent. In thirty of the fifty-three Wages Councils pay had risen more slowly. But this analysis does not take account of price increases during the period under study. In the twenty-three months – August 1968 to July 1970 – the Index of Retail Prices rose in twenty of those months. 'Thus workers who receive pay increases equalling the rise in the cost of living over the period, in fact, had their standard of living reduced throughout that period.'

We have now brought up to date this information, and have examined the increases in the minimum wage for each Wages Council against both price increases and the national wage index. This shows an improvement in that the minimum wage increases in only four of the Wages Councils, Retail Bread (Scotland), Wholesale Mantle, Paper Box and Road Haulage, failed to keep pace with the rise in prices up to March 1973. The position with wage rates appears even better in that only one Wages Council received a smaller percentage increase than the average over the thirty-month period. However, in money terms most of the increases were small and only appear impressive when measured against the very low minima at the beginning of the period. When the cash amounts are compared with average money increases they again show a deteriorating position.

ENFORCEMENT

The second distinguishing characteristic of Wages Councils is the power of inspection and enforcement. Wages Council inspectors have powers of entry to Wages Council establishments, the right to examine records and question those who they believe can help them to discover the facts. They follow up complaints from Wages Council employees as well as inspecting a random sample of businesses. An employer found guilty of failing to pay the amount laid down in a Wages Council order can be fined and made to pay the deficiency for a period of up to two years.

By the early 1950s, when the expansion of the Wages Councils had reached its peak, the number of inspectors settled at around 190 – 200. In 1954 the then Minister of Labour decided to economize on the cost of enforcing Wages Council orders by reducing the number of inspections from 7½ per cent of establishments to 5 per cent. By the end of 1955 the number of inspections was restored to 7½ per cent of establishments and the number of inspectors increased to 200. In 1958 the number of inspectors was reduced again and today their numbers total 142.

Commenting on this decline Baylis notes that:

'This reduction was less serious than that of 1954 because there was evidence to show that the need for enforcement through inspection was declining, and the number of establishments to be inspected was falling at a rate of about 1 per cent per year.'

Further:

'In most cases it is breaches of the minutiae of the orders rather than refusal to pay the basic rates laid down which form the large majority of offences.' (See F. J. Baylis, *British Wages Councils*, Blackwell,1962.)

(This is the most authoritative and detailed study on Wages Councils, but was published more than a decade ago.)

The remainder of this section looks critically at this statement and draws on a number of sources which suggest that underpayment is much more serious than most observers have so far suggested.

Table 2.7 opposite details the inspections carried out since 1968. It shows that over the last few years both the number of complaints and the number of inspections have fallen, although the number of establishments paying arrears rose in 1972. Likewise the number of workers paid arrears has fallen and, apart from 1972, so too has the amount paid in arrears. But what is clearly shown is that regularly about one in ten establishments inspected is found to be paying less than the legal minimum, and this total has remained constant for each of the years covered by the table.

This raises the question of how firms are selected for inspection. If this is done on a random basis, then it would appear that underpayment occurs in one in ten of all Wages Council establishments. If *all* Wages Councils were inspected in any given year, the total figure for recovery of funds would amount to around the £2 million mark. If, on the other hand, the sample inspected is not chosen on a random basis but past offenders form the basis of the sample, then it would appear that there is a large number of employers who regularly disregard the minimum wage regulations. Both possibilities are equally disturbing.

TABLE 2.7 Size of arrears paid to Wages Council employees

Year	Establishments on Wages Council lists	Complaints	Inspections	Per cent of establishments inspected	Establishments which paid arrears	Establishments paying arrears as per cent of total number of establishments	Per cent of establishments paying arrears as per cent of establishments inspected	Workers whose wages were examined	Workers paid arrears	Total paid in arrears	Average paid per worker
1968	498,902	8,792	50,905	10.2	8,795	1.76	17.27	265,370	13,417	177,930	13.26
1969	495,697	8,564	50,150	10.1	8,441	1.70	16.83	271,118	13,049	171,667	13.15
1970	485,373	8,136	53,941	11.1	8,081	1.66	14.98	262,281	11,928	157,898	13.23
1971	471,333	7,334	51,593	10.9	7,675	1.62	14.87	253,714	11,968	163,747	13.68
1972	464,960	7,483	48,507	10.4	9,048	1.94	18.65	235,720	11,213	220,084	19.62

Source: information from the Department of Employment.

51

LOCAL STUDIES

So far only national data have been presented on the underpayment of wages to employees in the Wages Council sector. A study by E. G. A. Armstrong (*British Journal of Industrial Relations,* 1966) shows that wide variations in underpayments also occur at a local level.

With the cooperation of the Inspectorate, Armstrong studied their records of inspections of Birmingham Wages Council establishments in 1962, 1963 and 1964. At the time unemployment was low – 1.7 per cent – and Armstrong was interested in finding out whether full employment in an affluent city automatically led to payment of at least the minimum Wages Council rates. His findings suggest that this does not happen; during the period under study, £14,445 of arrears were recovered for Birmingham workers, and of this £11,419 resulted from routine inspections. As the Birmingham research is the only detailed local study, and its findings are important for the argument we are developing, the main results are summarized in the following paragraphs.

Small establishments were the main, but not the only, offenders. 87 per cent of the establishments inspected employed fewer than eleven people. In total they employed 40 per cent of the inspected labour force, but accounted for 60 per cent of underpaid workers and 63 per cent of arrears paid. This led Armstrong to write: 'There exists a broad but definite inverse relationship between the size of firm and the frequency and degree of infraction.'

Concentrating attention on the smaller firms the Birmingham study attempted to predict the probability of workers being underpaid. By expressing the number of underpaid workers as a percentage of workers examined in firms for the four most important Wages Councils in Birmingham employing one to ten persons, the following 'underpayment odds' were disclosed.

TABLE 2.8   *Underpayment of Employees in Selected Birmingham Wages Council Industries*

Establishment	Per cent of workers underpaid		
	1962	1963	1964
Hairdressing	20	21	15
Retail Food	9	10	12
Licensed Residential Establishments	6	5	6
Retail Drapery	4	6	5

Source: E. G. A. Armstrong, *British Journal of Industrial Relations,* 1966

Commenting on these findings, Armstrong wrote: 'These chances of underpayment are much too high for there to be complacency about reduced Inspectors' activity.' With as many as one in five workers in Hairdressing being underpaid in two of the three years under study, it would be difficult to accuse Armstrong of an overstatement.

Armstrong also studied the percentage of workers underpaid for three of the main Wages Councils as well as the size of the arrears paid to workers. In Hairdressing establishments 55 per cent and 63.5 per cent of workers investigated were underpaid in 1962 and 1963 respectively. This dropped to 26.4 per cent in the following year, but in Retail Food the numbers underpaid were 45.9 per cent, 43.8 per cent and 46 per cent respectively, and in Licensed Non-residential Establishments the corresponding figures were 23.7 per cent, 27.1 per cent and 27.6 per cent.

It was in Hairdressing that evidence was found of underpayment in large establishments. For example, three firms employing 75 workers had their wage records examined. 59 per cent of the workers were found to be underpaid and 25 of these were receiving less than 90 per cent of their legally defined pay. The arrears repaid total £2,065.50 but none of the inspections arose from a complaint.

TABLE 2.9 *Arrears for Wages Council workers in Birmingham*

	1962	1963	1964
	£ underpayment		
Men	22.3	28.8	31.8
Women	27.8	35.2	44.1
Youths	49.0	50.7	16.9
Girls	33.4	32.3	21.0

Source: Armstrong, *British Journal of Industrial Relations*, 1966

Table 2.9 details the average payment of arrears to different categories of workers for the three years under study. As with all averages, extremes at both ends are merged, but it is important not to lose sight of how large some of the underpayments can be. In 1964, 29 women were paid arrears totalling £1,278. As Armstrong comments: 'A dramatic equivalent would be a lockout of such a labour force for four to five weeks, an event which would undoubtedly cause public comment and concern.'

There has been no other comparable local study to Armstrong's. There have, however, been odd pieces of information coming to light which suggest that the Birmingham study is far from atypical.

In April 1971 Nerys Williams conducted a small survey into the rates of pay of immigrant clothing workers in a Southall factory (*New Society*, 19 June 1972). Thirty-five contacts were made and of these twenty-five workers proved willing to supply information about their earnings. The working conditions described by Miss Williams warranted *New Society* to head the article 'The New Sweat Shops'. But not only were working conditions bad. Pay was extremely low and : 'Earnings of the group who had been at the factory for less than two years fell well below the statutory minimum,' which was then £11.10. No action was taken against the employer. 'During the mid-summer months of 1971 jobs were becoming increasingly difficult to keep and harder to find. Consequently, as no one was willing to lodge their grievances with the Wages Inspectorate, the contraventions go on.'

In cases where workers are unwilling to lodge complaints or are unaware of their rights, it is only by accident that anything is found out about the extent of underpayment. For example, the *Daily Telegraph* carried a report of a redundancy case (14 August 1971) where a pigkeeper had worked seven days a week for twenty-five years without a holiday and was paid £8 a week instead of the then legal minimum of £13.15 for a forty-two hour week. Although he was awarded his full redundancy payment, there was no mention of the payment of his wage arrears.

Fear of losing the only known form of employment was one reason why lace outworkers in Nottingham continued to work for well below the legal minimum. One worker reported working sixteen and seventeen hours a day and still earning less than £5 at the end of the week. And examples cited by employers of wages of £20 per week were found to be the earnings of a whole family undertaking outwork (Report by Liberal Party, March 1972).

Other evidence of underpayment was collected by the Liberal Party investigators in the south coast Hotel and Catering industry. Here a number of workers were receiving less than the legal minimum once the hours at work had been taken into account. And like their study of lace outworkers in Nottingham, no workers interviewed had complained to the Inspectorate, nor had the establishment been included in any of the Inspectorate's routine surveys.

POLICY IMPLICATIONS

This paper has looked at one in five of all workers in this country – the three and a half millions in Wages Councils and the one and a half millions in Public Administration.

Both groups of employment are characterized by low pay. It would be easier to raise the wage rates of the lowest paid in the public sector than the low rates of pay anywhere else. There need not be any unemployment effects providing we, the tax payers, are prepared to foot the bill and Nicholas Bosanquet in his paper outlines a policy for combatting low pay amongst public employees. The task, however, is more complex in the Wages Council sector.

It is clear from both the general data on minimum rates and earnings in Wages Council industries and the evidence on underpayment, that the majority of Wages Councils have failed to prevent the widespread occurrence of low pay in their industries. The claim of Guillebaud that the system 'has diminished to a marked degree the more extreme inequalities in wages different industries and within the same industry' is not supported by the available evidence.

However, in one or two Wages Council industries earnings have been raised considerably, for example in Road Haulage and Milk Distribution. The central factor in these successes appears to have been the strength of organization on both the employer's and trade union's sides. It is in those Councils where some degree of voluntary collective bargaining has become established that higher rates are observed.

This suggests that the crucial variable in determining the degree of low pay is the industrial structure, since this will determine the ease with which trade unions and, to a lesser extent, employers can organize. The work of J. Marquand supports this finding, as does a study which used regression techniques to analyse data from the National Poverty Study *(The Causes of Low Earnings amongst Manual Workers in Britain,* Stephen Winyard, University of Essex, April 1972).

The Wages Council industries where minimum rates

and earnings have remained low are those in which the average size of the firm is very small. Indeed in the whole of the Wages Council sector the average number of employees per firm is only seven. Nearly two out of three workers covered by Wages Councils are women and many work part-time. Two-fifths of the Wages Councils have a significant proportion of their labour force engaged as homeworkers. All these factors conspire to make trade union organization extremely difficult. In addition, it is sometimes claimed that the very existence of a Wages Council in an industry makes trade union expansion difficult. However this view is hard to reconcile with the successful organization that has taken place in some sectors.

Given this heterogeneity amongst Wages Council industries, a number of policy recommendations are appropriate. In those industries where voluntary collective bargaining has become established and earnings at the lowest decile are above 70 per cent of the average in that industry and where average earnings are not abnormally low, then abolition might be appropriate. This appears to be the approach in favour at present with the Government and seventeen Wages Councils are currently being considered by the Commission on Industrial Relations (CIR) with a view to either abolition or varying the field of operation.

Since 1947, fourteen Wages Councils have been abolished, the latest being Baking in 1971. In this industry effective voluntary bargaining had become established and minimum rates had been raised above those in all Wages Councils. However, when abolition is being considered it is sometimes evident that insufficient thought has been given to the lower paid workers in the industry. The CIR has recently proposed that the Industrial and Staff Canteens Wages Council should be abolished at a time when 49.3 per cent of its full-time female work-force is earning less than £14 and only 45 per cent of catering units are covered by collective bargaining arrangements.

It is important that any proposals for abolition should be linked to measures which will ensure that low pay does not persist or re-emerge in that industry. A minimum of 70 per cent of average earnings in the industry, together with continued inspection by the Wages Council Inspectorate might serve this purpose.

There are many Wages Council industries where voluntary collective bargaining is still a very distant objective and in these cases abolition is not feasible. The CIR has accepted this view and in its report on unlicensed places of refreshments states: '. . . the existing system of Wages Council will remain necessary in the foreseeable future.' (CIR Report No 36, 1973.) Such a recommendation is, in our view, disappointing since it could have been linked to a request to the Secretary of State for Employment to give some clear guidelines to the Wages Councils as regards the level for minimum rates. Given that some Wages Councils are to remain for the 'foreseeable future', then a programme to raise minimum rates, and hence earnings, should be introduced. This might set, as a target for Wages Councils, £22.50 for male workers and £14 for female workers, and these minimum rates should become operative (with allowances for the general movement in wages) in, say, three years.

One of the main arguments likely to be put against this proposal is that if rates are increased to any significant extent many workers will be made unemployed. However, as Guillebaud has pointed out:

'Experience has shown . . . that employers can be remarkably successful in the task of equating the marginal productivity of the workers to the wages they are called upon to pay.'

Another reform that is currently under consideration is to amalgamate Councils. It is perhaps typical of the

Wages Council sector that this proposal was made just over fifty years ago in the Cave Committee report on Wages Boards and only now is it receiving serious attention. Amalgamation would help to avoid the considerable duplication that occurs at present in, for example, the Retail and Clothing sectors. The assistant General Secretary of USDAW has proposed just two retail councils, one for foods and one for durable goods, and given that rates in the sector are currently set by only two Councils, with the others following, this suggestion makes good sense.

With a smaller number of Councils it would be easier to correct one of the weaknesses of discussion and negotiation in the Wages Council sector, the lack of information. It is suggested that a strengthened Wages Council secretariat should prepare annual reports on each Wages Council containing information on rates, earnings and employment in the industry and some comparisons with national trends in wages and prices. If the Councils were given a statutory responsibility to consider these reports then regular meetings would be ensured. This should in itself be a useful step given that employees in Wages Councils have in the past lost out because of the longer gaps between their increases compared with the private sector.

Our final proposal is far better enforcement of the minima. We have shown that there is evidence of underpayment on a wider scale than the national data suggest. There is a need for more inspectors and heavier fines. Indeed, the maximum penalty for paying workers below the statutory minimum is only £20, the same figure as in 1909. If the Government does not accept immediately the need for an increase in the number of inspectors, and continues to claim that underpayment is a minor problem, then we propose that in one year a number of blanket investigations are carried out in a few areas with the existing inspectorate. These would look at every Wages Council establishment in the chosen areas, and if they showed that payment below the minimum is on the scale we have suggested, then an increase in the number of inspectors is justified. However, even without these 100 per cent checks our estimates of something like £2 million per annum underpayment would indicate a need for around 250 Wages Council inspectors if the Government were to use the same ratio of inspectors to total amount recovered in the Wages Council sector as it does with supplementary benefits.

3. Immigrant Workers and Low Pay

David Stephen
Director of the Runnymede Trust
Director of the Industrial Unit

Most of the present Commonwealth immigrant population of Great Britain is the result of the influx of workers between 1955 and 1965. They were playing a specific role in changes in the structure of the labour force which were going on during the fifties and the early sixties in Britain. E. J. B. Rose has observed that 'the immigrant population is under-represented in those occupations normally considered most desirable, and over-represented in those occupations normally considered most undesirable.' (*Colour and Citizenship; A Report on British Race Relations,* OUP for IRR, 1969). In other words, the Commonwealth immigrant worker tended to enter those jobs, and those industries, which were failing to attract indigenous workers at that time, and which therefore, almost by definition, were 'socially undesirable'. Whether or not this notion of social undesirability includes pay as a principal component is not clear, but it would be reasonable to assume that monetary emoluments, and other than monetary emoluments, such as the availability of housing and social services near to the place of work, are the main determinants of what makes a job socially desirable in present day British society. The black population today may or may not suffer from low pay; but many of its problems derive from its situation as the outcome of a stopgap worker immigration into 'socially undesirable' jobs and districts in the fifties and sixties.

The data which would enable us to take this point

further is very sparse indeed. The most authoritative assessment that has been made of the role of immigrant workers in the economy, that of Jones and Smith *(The Economic Impact of Commonwealth Immigration,* Cambridge University Press, 1970) resorted to a largely impressionistic assessment of earnings characteristics of immigrant workers. Jones and Smith therefore simply looked at earnings in those occupations in which immigrants were concentrated. They did, however, quote a sample survey published in 1962 which found that Jamaican males were earning nearly 30 per cent less than the average for all male manual workers in Britain, and females some 20 per cent less than the average for all females.

There is some evidence that this gap has narrowed since, but it remains the case that immigrant groups, including the Irish as well as Commonwealth immigrants, have higher proportions of unskilled workers than does the total population. Similarly, in the semi-skilled groups all immigrant groups are over-represented in comparison with the host population. Stephen Castles and Godula Kosack *(Immigrant Workers and Class Structure in Western Europe,* OUP for IRR, 1973), using data from the 1966 Sample Census, placed immigrants in each of the seven main socio-economic categories followed by Rose. The lowest status groups for men were Jamaicans (94 per cent manual), Pakistanis (87 per cent), the rest of the Caribbean (84 per cent), Italians (84 per cent) and Irish (78 per cent). For women, the lowest status groups were Cypriots (82 per cent manual), Italians (80 per cent) and Jamaicans (74 per cent).

Yet it would be a mistake to conclude that coloured immigrant workers in Britain constitute a class as such, still less an identifiable 'under-class'. The numerical strength of the Commonwealth immigrant work force in Britain is such that nowhere, except in highly localised work-places or sections of industries, is it even a numerical majority. White workers predominate even in 'immigrant' jobs. Secondly, while the overwhelming majority of Commonwealth immigrants tend to be manual workers, considerable numbers of professional workers, particularly in the National Health Service, are Commonwealth immigrants. However, the Commonwealth immigrant population has certain other demographic characteristics peculiar to itself. Surveys have repeatedly shown that the age distribution of the immigrant population is markedly different from that of the population as a whole. The New Commonwealth population surveyed by the 1966 Sample Census had 47.2 per cent of its members in the twenty-five to forty-four age range; the comparable figure for the population as a whole was 25 per cent. On the other hand, the over-sixties made up 12.4 per cent of the population as a whole, but only 3.3 per cent of the New Commonwealth-born population. In addition, households of New Commonwealth origin tend to be larger than households of UK-born people; and the Commonwealth immigrant population lives in more over-crowded conditions. The average number of children in families, according to special tabulations done by Rose from the 1966 Sample Census, was 1.85 for the English born, 2.30 for the Pakistani-born, 2.35 for the India-born, and 2.43 for the West Indies-born. 20 per cent of English families, compared with 34 per cent of Pakistani families, 35 per cent of West Indian families and 36 per cent of Indian families had more than three children. The English had 2.66 persons for every 4.29 rooms, while coloured immigrants had 3.47 persons in 2.93 rooms. While the English were over-represented in rented unfurnished accommodation, coloured immigrants were grossly under-represented in local authority accommodation and rented unfurnished accommodation; 7 per cent of English householders were renting furnished accommodation in

1966, compared with 69 per cent of Pakistanis. In other words, low pay – if it does notably affect immigrant workers – would only be one factor in immigrant poverty.

The picture which emerges, therefore, is of a group which came in at the very end of the occupational scale, and migrated to the prosperous parts of the country to do vacant jobs in the fifties and sixties; but within those prosperous parts of the country, it entered the most congested areas, and tended to live in 'socially undesirable' areas in housing conditions worse than those considered as normal for the native-born population. Other factors differentiate the Commonwealth immigrant population from other groups generally described as low-paid. Bosanquet and Stephens, in their article 'Another Look at Low Pay,' (*Journal of Social Policy,* July 1972), cite the low earnings levels of older workers, and the fact that they tend to have high sickness rates, and are unlikely to have undergone training, and of unskilled workers, who suffer considerably more unemployment than other sections of the work force. Immigrant workers are rarely old; but they do tend to fall within the unskilled category.

Bosanquet and Stephens observe that there may be some movement into the unskilled group by people afflicted by temporary or permanent misfortune such as alcoholism or mental illness. Their view of the low-earning unskilled worker group is essentially of a group into and out of which workers move according to certain criteria. The question as far as immigrants are concerned, therefore, is whether those who entered the labour market at the unskilled level will remain there, either through discrimination or lack of qualifications. Yet, immigrants, according to Bosanquet and Stephens, 'will have more to offer in qualifications and abilities than British unskilled labour'. They are younger; their unskilled situation may be due to poor training opportunities in their countries of origin; and, in addition, as immigrants they may well be more highly motivated than the native unskilled.

The PEP Survey of Racial Discrimination in Britain in 1967 found that many immigrants were convinced that there is a colour bar in Britain.

'Some claim that employers will not take coloured employees at all; and that others will take them for only the most menial of jobs; that coloured people cannot hope for jobs at the level of their ability but have to settle for jobs that no-one else will do; that, in particular, they cannot hope for jobs of responsibility, influence or authority in society; and that consequently they are denied any opportunities for training and advancement; that, finally, they are sometimes exploited by employers who require them to do types of work, or work the long hours or accept low levels of payment they could not persuade white people to accept'. (W. W. Daniel, *Racial Discrimination in England,* Penguin, 1968.)

In other words, the pressures on immigrants to conform to a low status/low pay stereotype have been considerable.

FUTURE POLICY IMPLICATIONS – LOW PAY, BLACKS OR INNER CITY?

Any policy designed to deal with the phenomenon of low pay is likely to assist the majority of immigrants; another question, and a crucial one, (which we shall look at separately) is the role of immigration policy in the overall context of a low pay policy. Any policy which altered the structure of jobs, or which placed higher monetary value on occupations which are at present of low status and which involve substantial numbers of immigrants, such as hospital ancillary work, would have an important economic and social effect on the status of black people in British society. Many of the economic disabilities of Commonwealth immigrants, however, stem from other causes: large families – and the reluctance or inability of most housing authorities to provide suitable accommodation; discrimination in employment and housing; and the fact that areas of immigrant settlement are also areas of poor social provision and declining job opportunity.

Policies to improve the pay and status of black people – which is what race relations in Britain is about – or, put much more modestly, policies to guarantee that black people get the same opportunities as comparable whites, – presuppose a degree of flexibility in organizations like companies and town halls which it is not always realistic to assume. Few companies and few local authorities have made it clear that it is their policy not to discriminate, assuming that such declarations are either unnecessary or provocative. Yet in the present illiberal climate a positive initiative on race relations is not something that can be expected from the intermediate or low levels of large organizations without clearly enunciated directions from the top. But even before we can hope to increase the responsiveness of organizations, personnel managers and local authority officials need to be educated about race relations, simply with the object of showing them that policies designed to assist black people to participate fully in society are remedying underprivilege rather than imposing privilege. The bland assumption that to say 'we treat everyone the same' is to enunciate a sacred democratic principle – when in fact sameness of treatment in a situation of inequality is tantamount to approving and confirming that inequality – illustrates the magnitude of the educative task ahead. Until the basic climate is improved, to expect, for example, managers to promote qualified black people into positions of authority over whites is still, in most cases, hoping for too much. Similarly, mysterious processes in some local authority areas which confine black people to a small number of housing estates, rather than being distributed normally, will not be reversed until the basic climate improves.

On the other hand, the 'basic climate' – people's attitudes and ideologies – derive in the first place from the social situation in which they find themselves. In London the 'immigrant' areas have certain characteristics – they are in the inner area (with the exception of Southall), their population is declining, they suffer from acute housing shortages, schools have large numbers of probationer teachers and older teachers and a high staff turnover, and companies offering skilled employment tend to be moving out. The outer areas tend to be white, with a static or expanding population, a less acute housing problem, newer schools with more settled staffs, and expanding employment opportunities. The inner areas tend to have a wide range of social classes – from the very rich who are 'gentrifying' areas such as Barnsbury, to the poorest single-parent families or old people – while the outer areas tend to have a much more uniformly upper-working and middle-class population.

The dangers to race relations – indeed the growth of intolerance towards blacks and the poor generally – come from the white suburbs and not from the inner city. It is the outer London boroughs which refuse to assist with the inner area's housing problems. It is in the outer boroughs that racist and extreme right political groups are now seeing their greatest opportunities. Smug and fearful white ghettoes – fearful of what they would consider to be contamination by inner area poor people and blacks – are likely to conclude that blacks can only be poor and that therefore blacks cause social decay and bring deprivation in their wake wherever they go. And the managers who manage firms in immigrant areas, the officials who deal with the social security, employment and legal difficulties of immigrants, will all tend to come from those classes and those areas which are most hostile

67

to black people. Put differently, myths about Pakistanis and blacks thrive where there is no reality to compare them with, not in the inner city.

The breaking down of the seemingly inexorable social laws which are apparently polarising our cities in this way is the first step in changing attitudes. This is a major planning issue, but it must go hand in hand with the type of attitudinal or institutional change we alluded to earlier. To give an example: youth unemployment is much higher in Lambeth or Camden than in Richmond or Harrow (figures in May 1972: 166 and 77, compared with 35 and 31) because Lambeth and Camden are areas which firms are leaving, while Richmond and Harrow (according to the Greater London Development Plan) will be providing 11,000 and 3,000 new jobs respectively in the period 1966-1981. But there is a negligible coloured population in Richmond and Harrow: the coloured youth unemployed in May 1972 were 61 and 7 in Lambeth and Camden, but 3 and 1 respectively in Richmond and Harrow. The man in the street, not being aware of underlying social trends, will assume that there is youth unemployment in Lambeth because the people there are black; while the black youth himself will draw roughly the same conclusion though with a different emphasis (i.e. I am unemployed because I am black; white people in Richmond are not victims of racism).

The urban problem – the concentration of deprivation and low pay in inner urban areas – will become much harder to solve if the racial dimension becomes pre-eminent and obstructs rational analysis. Racial conflict locates the blame for an inequitable status quo in people's ethnic characteristics, rather than in politics, and is destructive. In other words, the question of inner city poverty should not be tackled on the basis of race; but must be tackled with new vigour – involving government intervention over the heads of local authorities – in order to prevent race from diverting attention from the real issues and providing an alibi for social inequality and segregation.

IMMIGRATION AND LOW PAY

Quite apart from problems arising from the low social and economic status of black people in our society is the question of future immigration policy. At present, government policy is to grant no work-permits for unskilled or semi-skilled workers except in the hotel and catering industry and for domestics. The fact remains that 'low pay' in Britain, exchanged into rupees or pesos in India or the Phillipines, represents a comparative fortune to the masses in those countries, many of whom are forced to migrate in order to survive.

Although some trade unionists have always justified their hostility to Commonwealth immigrants by alleging that they force wages down and act as scabs and black-legs, there is no evidence that immigrants have specifically fulfilled this function. It has always been the case in Britain that no Government has tolerated differential wages for workers from overseas. The Immigration Rules under the Immigration Act 1971, for example, make it quite clear that work permits will not be issued to persons who are not patrial unless it is shown that no local labour is available for a job and that pay and conditions are no less favourable than those offered to comparable local labour. (Indeed, trade union keenness to ensure equal treatment has sometimes resulted in an ending of specific incentives offered to immigrant workers. For example, the Transport and General Workers' Union opposed in the late fifties the payment of special bonuses to West Indians recruited in Barbados if they stayed with London Transport a certain period of time; this bonus was at first banned and then extended to all workers.) It may be the case that there are a certain number of illegal immigrants working in the sweat-shops and small establishments who are traditional wage cutters; but their numbers must be small, and their situation may have something to do with their weak legal and constitutional position.

It cannot be said that Commonwealth immigrants have entered specifically to keep wages down. Indeed, one survey (Cohen and Jenner, 'The Employment of Immigrants; a case study within the wool industry,' *Race,* vol. X, no. 1, July 1968) came to quite the opposite conclusion. Immigrant workers in a northern woollen mill were actually assisting modernization because they, unlike British workers, were prepared to keep machinery going at inconvenient times. There was, in other words, a correlation between modernization and the arrival of immigrants and a clear connection between expansion in certain industries and the introduction of immigrant workers, which – inasmuch as it implied adaptability and modernization rather than collapse of an industry in a difficult situation – ran counter to the 'immigrants as blacklegs' theory. Neither could it be said that where immigrants are concentrated in large numbers in a given plant or factory then wages which are low may not necessarily be those payable to comparable indigenous labour because comparable indigenous labour does not exist and there is no comparison. The numerical feebleness of the immigrant population in general has prevented any such situation (although in other Western countries, such as Germany or Switzerland, where there are very many more immigrant workers than here, such cases appear to be quite frequent; again, compared with Switzerland, many people doing 'foreign workers' jobs' are white and British.)

A variety of factors, therefore, among them pay, sucked in immigrant workers to Britain in the fifties and sixties and yet simultaneously there was unemployment in the British regions. If, instead of recruiting busmen in

Barbados from 1955 onwards, London Transport had opened a recruitment office in Newry or Gateshead, then it would be fair to suppose that, despite the relatively attractive wages which bus and Underground staff could be offered, there would be few takers despite continually high unemployment in both those areas. Both those areas possess, however, features which central London does not; housing is cheaply available, and the council housing stock is good, congestion is less, and the general pace of life is slower. These characteristics are the ones which decide whether or not people who may well be unemployed or earning very low pay will migrate to areas where their ability to enjoy the same standard of living might be debatable. Large scale investment in the social furniture of Inner London in the fifties might have made it an attractive proposition for the unemployed from the British regions to come to London to enter service industries. But British society was unwilling to pay the cost of that social investment, and so immigrants from societies where social provision was less, and who had both high expectations and ignorance of the level of social provision in Britain, entered the country to do those jobs. In the case of other occupations, such as labourers in textiles or foundry work, or clothing machinists, other features still have contributed to the departure of substantial segments of the native labour force. Inconvenient hours and unpleasant working conditions in the textile and foundry industries, rather than the levels of pay, have resulted in a number of plants having concentrations of immigrant workers. In the clothing industry, the style of supervision in many factories has produced the same effect.

W. R. Böhning, a German expert on European migration questions, has argued that the arrival of immigrant workers in the economies of Western Europe in fact impeded the re-ordering of the work force hier-

71

archy which might otherwise have taken place. In other words, the availability of unskilled or semi-skilled workers from overseas enabled trade unionists and employers to preserve a basically inequitable hierarchy when, otherwise, faced with a shortage of unskilled workers and an unwillingness of indigenous labour to undertake unskilled work, a radical re-organization of the structure of the work force might have been necessary. Put more concretely, Böhning would argue that the rigid divisions, in, shall we say, a hosiery mill between the elite and highly paid fully-fashioned knitters on the one hand, and the essential but semi-skilled and less well-paid bar-loaders on the other, would have broken down had it not been for the importation of Asian workers in large numbers into the industry in the early 1960's. Faced with the simple fact that no further bar-loaders were available, employers and unions would have had to re-design the work in hosiery mills so that the skilled workers would have to do their share of menial and unpleasant jobs. In such a hypothetical situation, the effects on pay would have been considerable, according to Böhning. If we assume that the amount of money available as wages to manual workers remained more or less constant, then there might well have been an up-grading of semi-skilled workers and a down-grading of the status of skilled workers, which would have resulted in a general levelling out of working class wages.

It is interesting to reflect that, alone among European governments, the British Government is now pursuing a strict policy of restricting the admission of unskilled foreign and Commonwealth industrial workers. In Germany, it is estimated that the total number of migrant workers needed in 1973, in addition to the 2.25 million already there, will be in the region of half a million. Immigrant workers constitute 5.1 per cent of the workforce in the old EEC; including 8.3 per cent in Germany.

In Britain, on the other hand, despite regional unemployment, some employers such as sections of the clothing industry, have complained that the Government's ban on work permits is hitting them hard; we have seen the grossly over-publicised but nevertheless significant incident of the importation of sewing machinists from the Philippines to work in a factory in Rochdale. Strangely enough, therefore, the British Government's anti-immigration policy, conceived in response to political rather than rational economic pressures, could result in Britain being forced to solve an issue which has been ducked by other Western European societies.

Recent Marxist analysts, such as Castles and Kosack, take the Böhning thesis further. They argue that Commonwealth immigrants and workers from the Third World in general provide what Marx called a 'reserve army of workers' who can be called upon at any time to enter the labour market of Western countries in order to keep working class wages and conditions low. Furthermore, they argue, the role of immigration is essentially to keep working class people divided by playing off the newly created white 'labour aristocracy' against the newcomers who tend, as we have seen, to do low status jobs and generally to be persons held in low esteem by the community.

Perhaps both Böhning and the Castles, however, underestimate the influences of other factors on job hierarchy. In Britain the role of trade unions in preserving differentials and maintaining the vast gulf between the lowest and the highest paid manual workers is at least as significant as the effect of immigration. Certainly the effect of immigration on British workers will in any case be far less in magnitude than the effect on German workers.

Because racists have tended to concentrate on the divisive factors in race relations, socialists, liberals and others have stressed the unity of the working class, and tended to defend worker immigration. In the light of recent research by Böhning and the Castles, such an approach may have to be regarded as over-simplified. Where immigration of unskilled workers from Third World countries takes place to any extent, it can have profound influences on the lowest paid in the developed countries, although at the same time it bolsters and upholds the high status of skilled, professional and other workers. Immigration, according to these criteria, could therefore be said to be against the interests of the lowest paid.

However, against these radical anti-immigration arguments, one could cite two other lines of argument. Firstly, there is the question of whether or not individuals in the Third World should be able to seek the opportunity to advance themselves by migrating to an industrial Western society. This argument can of course be countered on the grounds that the notion of 'advancement' is spurious and that what awaits the Third World worker may be a slight comparative improvement in standard of living but is in fact virtual helotry within the society which receives him; while Marxists will answer that individual advancement is merely a diversion from, and an undermining of, basic class struggles.

A second point is that for trade unions or a working class political party to oppose immigration may easily be misrepresented as opposition to immigrants as such. We all know that societies such as the 'Immigration Control Association', purporting to be concerned about the merits of British immigration policies, in fact frequently act in a way which would lead one to conclude that a better name for them would be the *Immigrant* Control Association'. The Right can frequently justify racism by reference to apparently permissible debates about immigration. The Left can fall into the contrary trap. Rather than consider the possible merits of a restrictive immigration policy, it tends to argue that since opposition to immigration is a racist position, anti-racists must be in favour of immigration. In fact, the low level and high emotional content of the public debate on immigration policy in this country has prevented an honest dialogue about the real issues involved.

Immigration of a wider spectrum of workers, i.e. immigration into the highest as well as into the lowest positions in the social hierarchy, might be a different matter. Immigration of poor workers with identifiable ethnic characteristics breeds social disharmony and division simply by their being correlated with poverty and poor social conditions. But it would certainly appear to be the case that the immigration of poor and unskilled workers from the Third World, particularly if that immigration is apparently 'controlled', has not been in the interests of the mass of workers in Western Europe. We must avoid repeating the situation of Switzerland, where labour immigration has resulted in a strangely inverted form of colonial exploitation, in which the 'superior' race, instead of imposing its rule on foreign peoples in faraway territories, imports the inhabitants of foreign territories and imposes its rule on them in its own country.

None of this is to deny that the development of the Third World and the huge gap between the economic situation of the Third World and the First World, are subjects which demand the most urgent attention. It is simply to say that in the present division of economic power in the world, the poorest in the richest countries are not well served by the importation of unskilled workers from poor countries, just as those countries themselves are not served by being denuded of some of their potentially most able and articulate workers.

4. Low Pay and Collective Bargaining

David Layton

Director of Incomes Data Services Ltd.

SOME REASONS FOR SCEPTICISM

There is a lot of scepticism about whether collective bargaining can do anything to raise the pay of the lowest paid workers. Let us look at a few of the arguments sometimes put forward.

Some point out that collective bargaining was not able to establish equal pay for women – even though obviously women were by far the largest group of lower paid workers. They go on to say that the Equal Pay Act is now having a sharper impact by setting new standards for women in many areas, so why not legislate for low pay as a whole, as has been done in many other countries?

A series of groups argue, from different standpoints, that patterns of distribution of pay, taken over the years, show very little change and much similarity in different countries. They argue that this is likely to continue and that there are fundamental reasons, social and economic, causing this. This pessimistic view very easily becomes the fatalistic view that it is no good trying to raise the pay of the low paid at all.

Another group takes the shorter practical view that whenever agreements push up the pay of the lower paid, this is followed by demands by the higher paid for equivalent or bigger increases to offset them. This produces the same differentials as before, so that the operation is self-defeating.

Next come those who have noticed that the same industries in many countries are found at the bottom of the table of low paid industries, and that they are found there whether there are minimum rates established by law or not. Typically we find in most countries a number of service industries, such as hairdressing and laundry; a large part of distribution; the textile industry; and of course agriculture. They say the odds are that this will continue.

Finally we have a sociological argument that there will always be a hard core of low paid. It consists of those who do not get paid reasonably because they are not capable of earning a living. It is argued that if you push up the pay of such workers you will drive them into unemployment. If these workers are to be paid more, then they have to be more efficient, or to be retrained. In practice what happens is that when they are given the opportunity it is found that they are disinclined, or are incapable, of making the effort required, often because of age or habit, and they opt out.

Such are some of the brief arguments advanced to explain why the poor are always with us, or to suggest that in any case collective bargaining has shown little evidence of setting the problem straight. There is some strength in several of them, but the arguments are very difficult to prove or disprove. What this paper proposes to do is to look at collective bargaining in some detail, bearing some of the arguments in mind, but with the object of picking out some steps that might be useful.

COLLECTIVE BARGAINING FIXES PAY FOR MANY PEOPLE

In the first place we have to recognise that for a great many people collective bargaining does it fact fix pay and the terms and conditions of employment, and it is certainly not the view that collective bargaining should only

do this for the higher paid. Many would feel that collective
bargaining is an operation of social and political importance, because it has the job of protecting the lower paid,
as well as dealing with the relationship between employers and employees as a whole. They certainly would
think that it is the job of the trade unions in the UK to
deal with the low pay problem if they possibly can. They
would argue that it would be a mistake to take away this
responsibility by settling the pay of employees through
legislation. The view is strongly held that free collective
bargaining is a good thing in itself, because it produces
important relationships between employers and employees and resolves problems, and they feel that employers ought to have to pay reasonably adequate rates,
as agreed with their workers.

The possibility of dealing with the low pay problem
by collective bargaining was not considered by the
Department of Employment and Productivity in its
inquiry into a national minimum wage, which was prepared in 1969. ('A National Minimum Wage – An Inquiry'
– *Department of Employment and Productivity*, HMSO,
1969.) It is a pity, because that inquiry is an important
reference work and it is precisely this possibility that is
the most important alternative to that of a national
minimum wage. It is this issue that needs to be investigated closely before handing the job over to be dealt with
by a minimum wage, negative income tax or any other
legislative scheme.

Hidden away in a dark corner, that report did however
point out that in Denmark, Norway and Sweden low
paid workers had been well protected by collective bargaining and that in the Netherlands, in practice, the
minimum wage (quoted at £14 14s. approximately in
1969) had been fixed by the process of bargaining – the
Minister giving final approval and ensuring its enforcement. Since then the system has been changed in the

Netherlands. The minimum wage (male or female) is now fixed and modified according to a formula – and not by process of bargaining. From Jan 1973 at DfL 216.90 (Approx. £30 at current exchange, though worth far less). In the Federal Republic of Germany it was also pointed out that a law dating from 1952 enabled a statutory minimum wage to be prescribed in a specific trade or industry, but that it had not been used. All classes of worker in fact had benefitted from the combination of powerful trade unions and the shortage of labour. So in any case collective bargaining had been a success in some places.

So what we have to do is to see what the possibilities are for dealing with the problem in the UK. This paper looks at the actual processes of collective bargaining in different industries and companies in the public and private sector. It notes the problems in low pay industries and in small as well as large businesses. It considers the special problems under 'severe' rising prices. It looks at differentials and at the sort of terms that have been negotiated recently and assess what might be done by collective bargaining within an imposed incomes policy.

NEGOTIATING FOR THE ELITE

Surprisingly, perhaps, it seemed a good idea to start with the most successful bargainers to see what they have done and are doing. We look, therefore, first at the bargaining which takes place around the status and pay of skilled workers – either at plant, company or national level (and perhaps this would be a good idea in other industries). We find that in engineering, printing and electrical contracting this is the hub of the negotiations and that there are many other industries where the same takes place. Here the unskilled and semi-skilled are carried along by the craftsmen's rates. None of these

79

industries would appear in any list with a high proportion of low paid workers.

In engineering or printing, negotiators do not raise the pay of the low paid workers to use this as a basis for raising the pay of craftsmen and to maintain differentials. He does not get higher pay by leapfrogging by pressure starting from the bottom. There are leapfrog situations in the engineering industry, but they are usually rather complicated, and one of the crucial ones is the situation where there is rivalry between unions, particularly craft unions.

In these industries the low paid are exceptional. There are, however, some pockets of low paid in almost all industries, and in a large group like engineering there are quite a sizeable number. Their problem is unlike the problem in industries where there is generally a low pay profile, which we shall come to later.

It does not seem that steps to raise the level of pay of the lowest paid workers need to be followed by a general raising of pay levels throughout the rest of the industry because of the squeezing of differentials. It is probably true that if the Engineering Employers' Federation and the Confederation of Shipbuilding and Engineering Unions thought that low pay was a top priority problem they could eliminate it without difficulty. The main effort would have to impinge on smallish firms often in regions with generally low pay levels.

We may usefully note that recently there has been considerable narrowing of differentials in percentage terms within certain large companies. Flat rate increases have been negotiated at Fords, Vauxhalls and Chryslers in the last two or three sets of negotiations. The pay is high, compared with many other companies. The lowest paid worker in the BLMC Leyland Bathgate negotiations in January 1972 had a rate of £32.29 for a normal working week. This is away above the national minimum rate in engineering. Differentials would not be a central problem. It is as well to recognise in passing that if one is hunting for a national job evaluation scheme one would find this sort of pay structure a very difficult problem.

THE PUBLIC SECTOR PRESENTS ANOTHER PICTURE

Unlike engineering, we note that in the public sector negotiations determine precisely the pay of employees in each industry or group. There may be bonus schemes; there may be some local arrangement; there may be over-time and shift work; but there are definite and precise grades, with rates for the job carefully applied. Often the minimum rates are well above those in the private sector, but it is most misleading to make comparison of the minimum rates negotiated in a public sector industry with the minimum rates laid down by joint industrial councils or wages councils for the private sector. These latter are often very different, for the minimum rates may be far removed from the normal rates of pay actually paid in companies.

The habit of using comparisons for determining pay for much of the public sector has precluded local author-ities or the Government from dealing with the problem of low pay on its own merits. This is rather silly, for there is more scope in the public sector to take a grip of it in many parts of the private sector. There is no reason why low pay should not be abolished in the public sector by the normal process of collective bargaining to ensure normal and reasonable rates of pay. The main failure is a lack of intention or a feeling that there really is no problem. The earnings figures, however, tell a different story.

In practice there are certain sectors of the public sector where we find strong collective bargaining and a totally different situation. The electric power and coalmining industries are good examples. In both cases the low paid worker is carried along by the skilled worker in the industry and by strong unions. In passing it is relevant to look at coal mining because of the special nature of the terms negotiated. After the Wilberforce Inquiry in 1972 the minimum unskilled worker's pay went up from £18 to £23, and in March of this year to over £25. For the underground worker (in 1972) the increase for the lowest grade was £6, in order to give an increased special differential for working underground. On the other hand the increase for the skilled underground worker on the highest rate was only £4.50, bringing his top rate at the time for five shifts to £34.50 (now £36.79). In the last negotiations a flat rate increase under Stage II was negotiated for all workers, and so there was no widening of cash differentials.

MINIMUM PAY AND CONDITIONS IN THE PRIVATE SECTOR

There are some hundred or more groups, or industries, in the private sector which negotiate in different ways about the minimum pay and conditions for unskilled workers, and about the rates for other grades. In some cases they merely agree the new minimum rates or terms and publish them – for instance in some wages councils and in some joint industrial councils they do not refer to the amounts of the changes. In other cases negotiators negotiate changes – the increases that all companies are going to apply. In some industries the process of negotiation is highly efficient and well organised, so that they fix not only minimum rates but structures and levels and conditions which are applied closely by all the member companies, but this is rare.

The differences between them reflect the different responsibilities that are carried by the employers and union negotiators in each of these negotiating bodies. It must therefore be open to question whether the less effective negotiating groups can be expected to be very effective over the particular question of low pay, unless inducements or pressures are applied from outside to stimulate action. They will not do it themselves, because their constituent members do not ask them to do it and do not expect them to do it. Only a detailed analysis, industry by industry, could sort out what particular new arrangements might be useful. One would not need to bother about the chemical industry, tobacco, oil, and other such prosperous industries, but amongst the smaller industries investigation needs to be done in detail. We can only touch on it here.

From time to time either a PIB or a Royal Commission or a joint TUC/CBI inquiry looks at what joint negotiating councils are doing, but almost invariably they generalise their comments and do not chastise or pillory the inept, neither do they give massive aid and support to the inadequate and heavily handicapped. It is not at all obvious that the collective bargaining arrangements in some of these industries are likely to develop strong and effective characteristics from within to do the sort of job needed for the employees, or for that matter, the employers.

THE LOW PAY INDUSTRIES

The toughest low pay problem is in the group of low pay profile industries and our first job is to see which they are. The test we apply is to look at those in which a high proportion of workers were earning less than £18 a week in April 1972 or/and a high proportion less than £25.

Data are taken from the Department of Employment's New Earnings Survey November and December 1972.) We only look at the men and we only look at those who worked at least a normal week in the week which included 19 April 1972. These statistics excluded all those whose earnings were reduced for one reason or other because they did not in fact do an ordinary week's work, e.g. for sickness or absence or as part-timers. As our interest is in collective bargaining we have in the main taken the information by negotiating groups, but a few are groups under their standard industrial classification grouping. The earnings figures include overtime, bonuses, shift pay and so on, but not special bonuses or back pay that happen to be received during that week.

The groups below employ relatively large numbers of employees, but there are quite a number of smaller industries for which the sample was really to small to provide separate data, so we do not find anything in the statistics about quite a number of minor negotiating groups, such as laundry or hair dressing. The rates of pay, if not the earnings, can be picked out from any publication giving the pay and negotiations of wages councils and joint negotiating councils. The data we are here looking at are not minimum rates of pay, but earnings in a full week. (Note: Similar sorts of lists are to be found in Appendix V of the D.E.P. Inquiry referred to elsewhere).

This listing shows the industries where there is low pay as a whole, but if we had taken the industries according to the numbers of workers in those industries who were on pay below the £18 or £25 level, we should have included quite a large number of other large groups. We should amongst others have included engineering, building, road haulage, timber and furniture, and a general group called 'other manufacturing industries'.

What strikes us in the list below is the importance of the textile and clothing industries. Then there are the large numbers in retail and wholesale distribution and the very considerable group in the public sector. Additionally there is agriculture, and we also have the catering industries which are rather special because of allowances in kind for accommodation and food. Indeed, quite a high proportion of the low paid workers in all sectors may be residential.

Industries with high percentages of Manual Workers earning less than £18 or £25 in full week in April 1972

	Union Represented	Percentages below	
		£18	£25
Cotton and man-made fibres spinning and weaving (JNC)	N.U. Textile & Allied W. Amalg. Assn. of Operative Cotton Spinners & Twines. Northern Counties Textile Trades Assn.	9.9	42.5
Leather & leather goods. SIC (XIV)	Produc. GMWU: NJWB – Nat. U Leather w. etc. Amal. Soc. Leather w. etc.	4.6	40.4
Made-up textiles (Wages Council)	M.U. Tailors & Garment w. TGWU	4.2	28.7
Woollen and worsted spinning and weaving (Yorkshire) JNC	Nat. Assn. of Unions in the Textile Trade	5.1	36.2
Clothing SIC (441-446, 449)	N.U. of Tailoring & Garment w.	10.1	40.9
Motor vehicle retail and repairing (UK)	AUEW: TGWU: GMWU: EETPU: N.U. of Sheet Metal w. etc.)	5.5	41.9
Wholesale Distribution SIC (810-812)	USDAW +	8.4	37.8
Retail co-operative societies (JNC)	USDAW: TGWU: GMWU: APEX: United Road Transport w.	6.2	42.4
Retail meat trade (JNC)	USDAW: TGWU:	7.0	50.3
Retail multiple grocery (England & Wales) (JNC)	USDAW:	7.4	32.6
Retail book selling and stationery (Wages Council)	USDAW: Retail Book Stationery & Allied Trades Employees Assn.	6.0	28.0
Retail drapery, outfitting and footwear (Wages Council)	TGWU: USDAW:	11.8	47.0
Retail food trades (Wages Council)	TGWU: APEX: USDAW: United Road Transport Union	8.3	43.4
Retail furnishing (Wages Council)	TGWU: USDAW:	8.6	43.5

Public Sector	Union Represented	£18	£25
Local Authorities (E & W)			
General and Clerical	NALGO: NUPE: COHSE: TGWU: GMWU:	(2.5)	41.3
Manual	NUPE: TGWU: GMWU:	(1.0)	49.2
Building	UCATT: TGWU: GMWU: EETPU: Amal. Soc. of Wood-cutting Machinists.	(2.2)	38.8
Government industrial establishments	13 unions	6.2	35.7
National Government services (SIC)		9.0	49.7
National Health			
Nurses and midwives (Whitley Council)	(12 unions)	6.6	41.1
Ancillary workers	NUPE: COHSE: TGWU: GMWU:	(2.1)	41.3
Educational Services (SIC)		8.5	67.1
Agricultural Wages Board (England & Wales)	NUAAW: TGWU:	16.7	60.6
Agricultural Wages Board (Scotland)	TGWU:	14.5	64.3
Catering (Licensed Non-residential) (Wages Council)	TGWU: USDAW: GMWU: & others – N.U. of Club Stewards: Amalg. Licensed Victuallers Soc. (Mgr. o Section: Nat. Fed. of Licensed Victuallers: Golf Club Stewards Assn: United Fed. of Hotel Magrs & Club Stewards of GB: London & District Magrs Licensed Victuallers Assn.	19.7	65.0
Catering (Licensed Residential) (Wages Council)	TGWU: GMWU: USDAW:	37.8	64.6
Property owning management (SIC) 863		23.3	71.7

It seemed of interest to note the unions represented on the joint negotiating groups. The unions concerned are only too well aware of the limited strength that they have in several of the sectors concerned.

However we wish to go about it we really have to face up to the real issue as to whether we do want to see *most* of the workers in these industries paid considerably higher wages. You cannot just put up the minimum rates. You have to face the central problem of the economics of these sectors.

SMALL VERSUS LARGE COMPANIES

Much of what we have to say about collective bargaining in these sectors and others has a direct bearing mainly on large companies. It is probably true that whatever might be required to deal with low paid workers can be coped with by almost all companies employing more than 100 people. The problems are, however, rather different in smaller firms or businesses. Although the rates of pay in most small firms are probably precisely determined either by company or national collective bargaining, this does not help very much. Unfortunately there are considerable numbers where this is not so, particularly in the low pay industrial sectors. The problem is small companies might indeed be amenable neither to more effective bargaining, nor to legislation. They are often rather personal organisations; they may have bad records; they may be too busy; and for a thousand and one reasons the issue will not be raised or dealt with. There may be scope for action by employers' associations, in liaison with trade unions, to create better standards, but in the areas where there is relatively low pay one foresees great difficulty.

ARE DIFFERENTIALS THE KEY PROBLEM?

On the problem of differentials and on the question of what would happen if one established a national minimum wage the report of the inquiry by the Department was very cagey. Part VI was all about costs and other economic consequences. Most of it was based on hypotheses and what it actually said was 'there is therefore no clear guidance as to the size of the effect of a national minimum on the earnings of those who are not low paid'. What the inquiry did not do, and was not expected to do, was to look at what would happen to differentials if there had been a planned programme for negotiating higher rates of minimum pay, sector by sector. That is something that still needs to be done. Here we begin by looking at this question from a purely empirical viewpoint to see what negotiators appear to be doing at the moment.

The details of agreements made by a large number of companies and in particular industries in both public and private sectors are much more readily available than they were a few years ago. It is therefore possible to see exactly what companies negotiate and the terms and the changes they make – even if it is not possible to get accurate information about numbers of workers in different grades and about earnings. The notable feature of these agreements is their variety. They are not only different in different industries, but also as between different companies. As Nicholas Bosanquet also comments in his paper, it is astonishing to see the difference between the levels in the rates of pay for what may be regarded as similar jobs – for instance, cleaners, or craftsmen, or drivers, or clerks – and the differentials between the different jobs vary enormously, both in cash and in percentage terms.

There is no doubt that pay structures are a most important part of the social structure of companies. In some industries traditions are strong right across the board.

Differentials tend to get settled and accepted and sometimes get set in very firm patterns. On the other hand there are many examples where changes have been taking place they have not only been taking place because there have been flat rate increases for all, but also because of deliberate structure negotiations. Many companies either continuously or from time to time revise their structures to cope with changing situations. This is not obviously found to be associated with reaffirming previous differentials, indeed quite the contrary.

In many groups percentage increases of the same amount have been given to all manual workers, but in contrast there have also been others where flat rates have been agreed. Recently there seem to have been somewhat more flat rate increases across the board, giving smaller percentage increases to the higher than to the lower paid workers. In some cases there have been tapered percentage increases. Flat rates are not automatically found to be followed by percentage rates in later negotiations to counteract their consequences. Differentials have been squeezed in real terms.

Coming then to the question of low pay. Suppose we are talking about raising the pay of those below £18 up to over £20. It need not be assumed that this would have a serious general effect on the higher paid in industries in which the majority of workers are well paid. On the other hand, the situation is obviously much more difficult where the level of pay is low as a whole in a particular industry: very little squeezing of differentials would be acceptable. It is not obvious that we can accept the view that because of the problem of differentials we cannot deal with the low pay problem at all, and it would be wrong to assume that pushing up the pay of low paid workers is essentially a process for pushing up everybody else's pay. Most negotiations are naturally about cash increases and not percentage increases and at a time when the cash figures are in pounds a great deal can be done to narrow differentials in real terms. And that brings us to the problems caused by price increases.

PRICE MOVEMENTS AND COLLECTIVE BARGAINING

One of the main objectives of much collective bargaining in recent years has been to get enough pay increase to offset price increases, so no apology is made here for looking at this particular subject. It is not just an issue that is of interest to employees, for even where there is no collective bargaining employers have often given an annual round of increases to their staff to offset the cost of living.

In the past year or two the impact of prices on pay has been most disturbing and the erratic process has frustrated many trying to deal with the long term problems of facing collective bargaining. It has made all sorts of problems most difficult to handle, including negotiations about structures, piecework, productivity bargaining, and of course low pay. In practice pay increases have been granted to employees only from time to time, (many individuals often getting a pay increase only once or twice a year), whilst price increases have been going on all the time, and these price increases have in practice hit individuals in many places and in many groups much harder than the percentage movement of the Retail Price Index would suggest.

There has been a very unbalanced situation in which collective bargaining has been trying to offset sharply, steadily or erratically rising prices with steep increases only at long intervals. Even the biggest increases have seemed quite unsatisfactory very shortly afterwards because of the attrition of price increases – often in a manner seemingly very inequitable. It is not reasonable to expect to find therefore that the activities of unions to increase the pay of the highest paid or the low paid, would have fallen into any uniform significant pattern and they have not. The common objective to try and provide people with a stable standard of living in a situation in which prices have been moving so erratically has been quite impossible to achieve on a twelve months negotiation basis.

We fall into gross error if we start making comparisons of the movements of average earnings and the movement of the Retail Price Index and assume that as earnings have been going up faster than prices, standards of living all round have been improved. There has been no feeling of stability anywhere and in many cases a fall in standards for many, even comparing one year with another.

How far it is possible to offset price increases for people on different levels of pay, and how it ought to be done, is something that is going to be considered much more seriously in the months to come. There are all sorts of possible arrangements and whilst the idea of having automatic wages increases has not always been favoured by either trade unions or employers there is a very different situation now to be faced. Negotiating once a year just will not do if we are set for 8 per cent increases in prices.

The key way of protecting living standards is by aggreeing that wage increases should automatically be provided to offset price changes on a certain predetermined basis. Until the sixties there were quite a number of industries in the country which had some type of cost of living clause in their agreements. There are today many operated abroad. The Labour Government's incomes policy quite deliberately advocated abolishing them on the grounds that increased wages had to be earned from higher productivity. So in practice most of the arrangements were abolished and a percentage norm became the leading concept. At the time this view reflected the theory that if increased wages automatically followed

91

price increases, then that produced the inflation spiral. It is unfortunate that insufficient attention was paid to the crucial question of time lags in any such arrangement, and that even less attention was paid to the need for offsetting price increases to stabilise real wages. Now the wheel has turned full circle and almost everyone recognises that something must be done – either by threshold agreements to ensure that some portion of an increase is maintained in real terms, or by a straight cost of living scale to protect a given standard of living from being undermined by price changes.

The low paid employee has a special interest in such arrangements, because when prices rise he or she has to go without necessities, whereas the better off have no need to do so. It is important at the very least to stabilise an employee's low standard of living. It matters very much to the low paid worker that when prices are moving up anything like 5 per cent or 8 per cent as a whole (and for many individuals, therefore, very much more) something effective should be done quickly and often. The low paid worker needs either a pay review every six months or less to offset price increases, or an automatic arrangement. Such arrangements can be quite simply negotiated by joint negotiating councils or can be laid down by wages councils orders. The simplest arrangement is to provide for a pre-determined cash increase.

PROTECTION FROM SPASMODIC LOW PAY

We have just looked at the urgent need for the protection of the low paid worker against price changes. There is also a need to deal with the employee who suffers spasmodic reductions of pay to a very low level. It has always been known in companies that pay packets are somewhat erratic for a number of reasons; for example because of absence, or sickness; because workers are on shifts; or do overtime; because of short-time working; because of piece rates; because of job changes; and the like. A very recent set of statistics produced by the DE throws some light on this problem and the figures deserve close scrutiny in the context of low pay as a whole, so we go into them in some detail below.

The April DE Gazette analyses what happened to the pay of individuals who appeared in the New Earnings Survey samples in 1970, 1971 and 1972. Instead of just telling us about average earnings the Department has looked at the way in which the earnings of individuals have changed between each set of two years. What follows is about the earnings of full time employees. It does not include any information about those persons whose earnings dropped sharply because of absence or sickness, into the low earnings category.

Key tables show joint distributions for 1970/71 and 1971/72, distinguishing full time men and women, manual and non-manual. We quote the one for 1971/72 for manual men on Page 94.

The great bulk of the employees are moving up and down relatively small amounts more or less around the average movements of earnings as a whole, but there are some quite startling exceptions, and similar exceptions are found in the 1970/71 tables. We find, for instance, that one male earning between £50 and £60 in 1971 was earning less than £15 in the following year; whilst three earning under £17 in 1971 were earning more than £50 in 1972. Further analysis of the data done by the DE showed the age was not a very significant factor in explaining the different size of movements and that the same was true of overtime. Ups and downs were not due to overtime one year and not the next.

We look at the information in another way in the table on Page 95 which shows the joint distribution of changes in earnings between 1971 and 1972, against levels of earnings in April 1971:

TABLE 4.1 Joint distributions of gross weekly earnings in April 1971 and in April 1972 FULL-TIME MANUAL MEN, aged 21 and over

Range of earnings in 1971 (Note 1)	Range of Earnings in 1972 (Note 1)											
	Under £15	£15-£17	£17-£20	£20-£25	£25-£30	£30-£35	£35-£40	£40-£45	£45-£50	£50-£60	£60 and over	Total
Under £15	113	95	59	45	11	10	4		2		2	341
£15-£17	17	122	434	177	79	32	12	7	3	1		884
£17-£20	13	46	797	1,689	512	194	78	39	15	12	5	3,400
£20-£25	20	25	277	2,905	3,261	1,245	552	215	99	56	25	8,680
£25-£30	12	13	81	808	3,096	3,387	1,371	572	277	163	36	9,816
£30-£35	10	3	42	301	1,000	2,308	2,321	945	439	244	71	7,684
£35-£40	5	1	13	119	321	737	1,318	1,166	545	344	89	4,658
£40-£45	2	2	4	40	103	280	433	609	531	343	123	2,470
£45-£50		1	3	17	64	113	164	221	240	309	108	1,240
£50-£60	1	1	1	13	21	62	102	132	111	260	165	869
£60 and over			1	7	12	14	30	40	30	69	145	347
Total	193	309	1,711	6,121	8,480	8,382	6,385	3,946	2,292	1,801	769	40,389

Source: Department of Employment Gazette, April, 1973.

TABLE 4.2 Changes in Earnings between 1971 and 1972

Range of earnings in 1971 (Note 2)	Change of Earnings between 1971 and 1972 (Note 1)											
	Decrease of					No Change	Increase of					Total
	Over £20	£15-£20	£10-£15	£5-£10	£0-£5		£0-£5	£5-£10	£10-£15	£15-£20	Over £20	
Under £15				4	20	19	202	54	17	14	11	341
£15-£17			1	1	31	27	603	114	60	26	21	884
£17-£20			2	6	197	60	2,040	662	247	102	84	3,400
£20-£25		4	8	75	930	91	4,304	1,943	742	339	244	8,680
£25-£30		9	23	307	1,465	78	4,195	2,173	865	405	296	9,816
£30-£35	5	19	122	551	1,408	52	2,885	1,516	640	266	220	7,684
£35-£40	5	54	190	497	873	24	1,548	806	352	178	131	4,658
£40-£45	23	67	171	339	485	14	663	379	164	86	79	2,470
£45-£50	43	72	146	198	217	6	250	160	66	38	44	1,240
£50-£60	77	89	133	116	110	4	136	116	36	24	28	869
£60 and over	124	29	39	36	29	1	26	23	20	10	10	347
Total	277	343	835	2,130	5,765	376	16,852	7,946	3,209	1,488	1,168	40,389

Source: Department of Employment Gazette. April. 1973.

It is astonishing what a large number had increases or decreases as between the two weeks of over £10 per week – many at the bottom as well as the top.

It is clear from these tables (and others in the Gazette referred to) that some people got into the high brackets exceptionally and some people got into the low brackets exceptionally. What we do not know from this sort of statistical analysis is what on earth were the reasons. What we do know is that in the figures are people working on Payment-By-Results; on shifts; and on all sorts of bonus sustems. We know that some people may only get a guaranteed fallback rate when work is short, and we know that some people may earn very high wages for long or short periods. We know that some may change jobs – indeed the DE notes that there are ten million or more job changes each year.

What the figures tend to show is that we perhaps have not really understood in the past what the figures of average earnings really mean. In particular we should beware of assuming that the distribution of average earnings in any industry or group in a particular week provides a proper statistical basis for talking about dis- tribution of average gross earnings per year, or of not income after tax.

We give one further table from the Gazette that is interesting, puzzling and possibly enlightening. It shows the average changes in weekly earnings of men aged 30-39. Between the two weeks one in 1970 and one in 1971 the lowest paid workers on average had increases of over £5, and the highest paid workers had decreases on average of £9.

The patterns on the opposite page are particular to male manual workers and are not found in an analysis of what happened to the pay of women, manual or non-manual, nor what happened to the pay of non-manual men. None of them show this heavy number or size of decreases.

TABLE 5.3   *Full-time manual men aged 30-39: changes in weekly earnings, April 1970 to April 1971*

Level of earnings in 1970	Average increase 1970-71	Percentage increase 1970-71
£15–£17	+£5·3	+33·2
£17–£20	+£5·3	+28·4
£20–£25	+£4·8	+21·1
£25–£30	+£4·1	+14·9
£30–£35	+£2·2	+ 6·9
£35–£40	+£0·5	+ 1·3
£40–£45	−£1·7	− 3·9
£45–£50	−£4·7	−10·0
£50–£60	−£9·0	−16·3

Source: Department of Employment Gazette, April, 1973.

Now let us look particularly at the low pay end. The statistical information in the New Earnings Survey has been studied to show particularly what happens to the pay of individuals in relationship to the lowest decile group. Some percentage figures showing the changes are set down simply in the table below:

TABLE 4.4   *Full-time manual men working in April 1970, 1971 and 1972: numbers in relation to the lowest paid tenth*

Whether above or below £17·7 in 1970	£19·8 in 1971	£22·0 in 1972	Sample numbers	Percentage of total
(a) Above	Above	Above	23,103	83.2
(b) Above	Above	Below	756	2.7
(c) Above	Below	Above	654	2.4
(d) Above	Below	Below	463	1.7
(e) Below	Above	Above	850	3.1
(f) Below	Above	Below	267	1.0
(g) Below	Below	Above	369	1.3
(h) Below	Below	Below	1,290	4.6
			27,752	100.0

Source: Department of Employment Gazette, April, 1973.

The tabulation on the previous page shows that a number of people who are found in the lowest pay tenth are only in the lowest tenth in one of the three weeks. This suggests that those people's problems might well partly be handled by seeing that they have more regular pay when they do a full week's work than they have at present. Collective bargaining may have some useful part to play in looking at the form of pay arrangements and at the terms of pay guarantees. In addition it could also do more to ensure that those persons who are absent or are only perforce able to work less than a full week are paid an adequate wage. (Earnings of absentees are not shown in these statistics about full time workers).

Table 4.4 above also shows in contrast that there is a hard core of lowest paid workers who appear in the lowest tenth in all three years, or in two out of the three survey weeks. 8.6 per cent of full time manual workers – those shown by lines (d), (f), (g) and (h) – were in the lowest decile in at least two of the three survey weeks. This confirms the view that there is a chronic low pay problem and that it is not just a matter of people being low paid on a casual basis. The DE have promised to produce further analyses of the occupations, industries and ages of this hard core of low paid workers, as shown by the New Earnings Surveys, but it seems probable that the figures will bring to light very little that is not already known about the sectors of industry in which useful action is known to be needed and could be tâken. However, when they do come let's be ready to use them.

INCOMES POLICY FOR STAGE III AND IV WILL SET THE PACE

Whatever can be done in the near future will be severely circumscribed by the next stages of incomes policy. When it comes into effect it can either open the way for those engaged in collective bargaining to do things about low pay, or it can prevent them, or it can take over as a Government function – the cushioning of the low paid worker. Doing something about low pay has been part of the scripture of policies since the beginning. Under the Labour Government it had a special place during the period of severe restraint. It is found in all incomes policies – or almost all – abroad. During our recent freeze, to the extent that prices went up, it was the low paid that suffered most. Under the Second Stage – the method of flat rate plus 4 per cent – went very little of the way towards giving them preferential treatment. If prices and incomes policies are going to be at all effective in the future, then the method of helping the low paid could be most significant. Collective bargaining will not be allowed freely to choose its own solutions.

We have already suggested that arrangements should be made to encourage cost of living clauses or threshold agreements – to protect living standards – at least for the low paid. We have suggested encouraging negotiations also to ensure regular pay for low paid workers to overcome the problems of spasmodic penury. A third possibility is to provide that any pay increases negotiated for groups or individuals whose pay is below a certain level should fall within the accepted pay limits, as has been done recently in the USA. This would mean deciding on maximum figures. Additionally it would be possible to alter the present principles of allowable costs by permitting such pay increases for the low paid to be offset in full by higher prices, instead of partially, as under the present Stage II arrangements.

Perhaps more rewarding in the long run would be for the policy to be aimed at challenging unions and employers to make plans for the next four or five years to resolve the problems of low pay in their own particular industries. Essentially this would involve industrial groups in finding out first what their low pay problems really were. It would put the responsibility fair and square upon the employers and workers in the industries concerned to decide what to do. One of the essential features would be that proper statistics should be produced by the negotiating partners about the situation in the industries for which they are responsible. (This can already be done quite simply for companies by demanding the information in pay bill calculations). Low Pay would be a special case. The pay board could be expected to supervise and authorise plans and to insist that they are monitored.

Plans for the future should be called for, not only for the private, but also for the public sector, and the review plans for the public sector might well be used as an example. The best approach for an incomes policy is to put the problems of low pay as a challenge to the particular unions and employers directly concerned, rather than to propound a policy allowing for permissive increases without demanding a long term plan. By far the most difficult problems are those in the listed industries, given earlier in this chapter, where the whole profile of pay is low relative to that of most of the community. They will not disappear easily whether tackled by legislation or collective bargaining.

5. Low Pay and the Cycle of Poverty

A. B. Atkinson
Professor of Economics at the University of Essex

The aim of this paper is to consider the relationship between low pay and poverty in Britain. Twenty years ago such a paper would probably have been considered unnecessary, since it was widely believed that low pay played little or no role in causing poverty. Beveridge argued that:

'The social surveys of Britain between the two wars show that in the first thirty years of this century real wages rose by almost one-third without reducing want to insignificance, and that the want which remained was almost wholly due to two causes – interruption or loss of earning power and large families' (*Social Insurance and Allied Services*, HMSO, 1942, p. 154.)

and this view appeared to be borne out by Rowntree's third survey of 1950, which showed that low wages accounted for only one per cent of families below the poverty line (see column three of Table 5.1). This dismissal of low pay as a cause of poverty was, however, premature. Firstly, Abel-Smith and Townsend demonstrated in *The Poor and the Poorest* that, in fact, low wages were still important in 1960 (see column four of Table 5.1). As was confirmed by the government's *Circumstances of Families* report, there are men working full-time in their regular job who earn less than the amount required to keep even a moderate-sized family at the supplementary benefit level. Secondly – and less widely recognised – low pay is important not only as a direct cause of poverty but also as an *indirect* cause. It is with this latter aspect that the present paper is particularly concerned.

The indirect role of low pay as a cause of poverty arises in two (related) ways. The first concerns the inter-relationship between different stages in a person's life history – the fact that low pay at one time may be an important factor leading to poverty later in life. The figures shown in Table 5.1 simply represent a 'snapshot' at one point in time, whereas for an individual appearing in any particular category past experience may be just as important as the fact that he is now retired or sick. The inter-relationships between different stages of the life-cycle are most clearly demonstrated by poverty in old age. A pensioner is less likely to fall below the supplementary benefit level if he owns his own house, receives an occu-pational pension and has savings on which he can draw. Whether or not he is in this fortunate situation depends, however, on how he has fared during his working life. A low paid worker is rarely able to buy a house, he is less likely to be covered by an employer's pension scheme and his capacity for saving will have been severely res-tricted. It is quite possible, therefore, that low wages, while not a direct cause of poverty, prevent a person acquiring the assets necessary to raise him above the poverty line in old age.

The second way in which low pay plays an indirect role is that it is part of a more extended pattern of labour market disadvantage. (This point is developed in terms of the concept of a 'dual' labour market by N. Bosanquet and P. Doeringer, 'Is there a Dual Labour Market in Great Britain?', *Economic Journal*, 1973.) We need to interpret low pay more generally as low status in the labour market, and recognise that it is associated with other factors which may lead to poverty. Low paid workers are more likely to become unemployed. The jobs they do may lead to higher rates of sickness absence. They are less likely to enjoy fringe benefits such as sick pay schemes, occupational pensions. Interpreted in this way, low labour market status may be much more important as a cause of poverty than is suggested by the figures in Table 5.1.

The aim of this paper is to bring out this indirect role of low pay in the cycle of inequality and to argue that low pay cannot be viewed in isolation but must be seen as part of a wider process leading to the persistence of poverty from one stage to the next of the individual life-cycle. After a brief review of the evidence about low pay the paper examines the relationship between earnings and the life-cycle of need, presenting a modern version of Rowntree's famous diagram illustrating the 'alternating periods of want and comparative plenty.' It then goes on to demonstrate the inter-relations between low earnings and unemployment, sickness absence, and poverty in old age. The final section summarises the main implications of the analysis.

TABLE 5.1   *Percentage of those in poverty*

	1899	1936	1950	1960
Old age	1*	15	68	33
Sickness	2*	4	21	10
Unemployment	2	29	–	7
Low Wages	55	38*	1	32*
Large family (5 or more children)	22	5*	3	8*
Single parent family	12*	8	6	10

Note: * denotes estimated figures.

Sources: B. S. Rowntree, *Poverty: A Study of Town Life,* (pub. Macmillan, 1902)

1936 B. S. Rowntree, *Poverty and Progress,* (pub. Longman, 1941)

1950 B. S. Rowntree and G. R. Lavers, *Poverty and the Welfare State,* (pub. Longman, 1951.)

1960 B. Abel-Smith and P. Townsend, *The Poor and the Poorest,* (pub. Bell, 1965.)

LOW PAY AMONG MEN

For the purposes of this paper, low pay for men is defined to be weekly earnings below two-thirds of the median earnings of all adult men working full-time whose pay was not affected by absence, which for the past three years would have given the following figures:

	£ a week
April 1970	18.1
April 1971	19.8
April 1972	22.3

The important feature of such a definition is that the standard of low pay is related to the general level of earnings. The two-thirds figure can, of course, be varied but it was chosen partly on the grounds that it approximates the earnings of the lowest decile of full-time adult men (£21.9 in April 1972). This not only allows ready use of the Department of Employment earnings surveys but also means that the definition coincides in the case of current earnings with that adopted by the Prices and Incomes Board, who defined the low paid as those falling below the bottom decile. (National Board for Prices and Incomes, *General Problems of Low Pay*.) In what follows, the earnings of the lowest decile will be used interchangeably with the two-thirds figure as an indicator of current low pay, although it should be emphasised that the definition differs *in principle* from that adopted here, and would lead to quite different conclusions if the earnings distribution changed.

Who are the ten per cent who earned less than £22 in 1972? The question as to who are the low paid will be discussed at greater length in subsequent papers, but for the present analysis it is useful to have a preliminary look at the evidence from the New Earnings Surveys set out in Table 5.2.

TABLE 5.2 *Low Paid Workers (Full-Time Men Aged 21 or over) April 1972*

	Percentage with low pay	Proportion of total low paid (%)
All men	10.3	100
Non-manual	6.8	24
Manual	12.3	76
By occupation		
Unskilled manual in industry	25.2	20
Farming etc.	46.3	8
Catering, domestic and other services	45.1	8
By industry (manual workers only)		
Agriculture etc.	40.1	5
Miscellaneous services	33.7	9
Professional and scientific services	29.1	6
Public administration	27.7	8
Distributive trades	26.1	9
Textiles	14.6	3
Construction	12.7	9
Transport	6.4	5

Source: Department of Employment, *New Earnings Survey 1972.*

The first important point is that they are principally manual workers – nearly four out of every five low paid workers. If we consider the breakdown of manual workers by occupational and industry categories, then more than one in five low paid workers are unskilled workers in industry, and another 16 per cent are farm or service workers. The industries with large numbers of low paid workers are those which might be expected from the studies by Marquand and others, with public administration, services and distribution particularly prominent. (J. Marquand, 'Which are the lower paid workers?- *British Journal of Industrial Relations*, November, 1967, pp. 359-74.) Although the evidence presented in Table 5.2, suggests that low pay may be found in many different sectors of the economy, it is clear that there are certain groups which are much more likely to be low paid; and where there is only limited information about earnings it may not be unreasonable to focus particularly on the position of unskilled manual workers in industry, the service trades, the public sector and agriculture.

THE LIFE CYCLE OF EARNINGS AND NEED

Let us take the case of an unskilled male manual worker whose earnings at the age of twenty-one are at the lowest decile for all full-time male workers of that age (£19.50 a week in April 1972). What are his earnings prospects for the rest of his life and how are they related to his family responsibilities?

In predicting career earnings,* we have to make assumptions about:

(a) changes in the overall distribution of earnings,
(b) changes in the individual's ranking within the overall distribution.

In the former case, it is assumed that the shape of the distribution remains unchanged over time, as has broadly been the case historically, so that the earnings of each percentile remain the same proportion of the median. The second problem is a difficult one, since very little is known about changes in ranking over the working lifetime. The assumption made here is that he remains at the lowest decile of current earnings for the relevant age group, or that his career earnings are two-thirds of the median career earnings. This assumption is perhaps rather pessimistic. The evidence from a recent study showed considerable movement in and out of the bottom ten per cent: only half those below the lowest decile in

*Lifetime career earnings have frequently been discussed for professional workers (e.g. in Royal Commission on Doctors' and Dentists' Remuneration, Report, 1960) but less commonly for low paid workers.

1970 remained below two years later. ('Low Pay and changes in Earnings', *Department of Employment Gazette,* April 1973). This fluctuation in earnings means that there is less inequality in career earnings than in annual or weekly earnings. As a result, the worker with career earnings two-thirds of the median would be below the lowest decile for career earnings.*

The resulting pattern of lifetime earnings is shown by the heavy line in the upper part of Fig. 5.1, where all amounts are expressed in terms of April 1972 earnings levels. Typically, the earnings of low paid workers reach a peak early in their lives and then decline, and this pattern is borne out by the diagram, where earnings are at their highest in the 30s. In terms of the criterion for low current pay (£22 a week), earnings are above this level from age 25–49 and he falls below in his 50s. The importance of low pay among older workers has been brought out by N. Bosanquet and R. J. Stephens, 'Another look at Low Pay', *Journal of Social Policy, July, 1972.)*

The variation of earnings with age has to be viewed in the light of family needs at different stages of the life cycle. For this purpose, needs have been assessed on the basis of the supplementary benefit scale plus forty per cent (and rent), following the approach of Abel-Smith and Townsend, and on the following stylised life history of the family:

Age		
22½	One child aged 1	Wife not working
27½	Two children aged 3, 6	Wife not working
34½	Three children aged 5, 10, 13	Wife not working
44½	One dependent child aged 15.	Wife earning £4 a week
54½	—	Wife earning £4 a week
62½	—	Wife retired
65	Retired	

*This illustrates the importance of distinguishing between the P.I.B. definition of low pay and that adopted here.

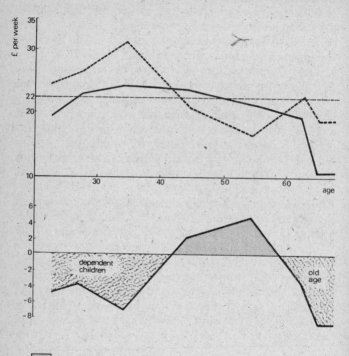

earnings exceed defined needs

earnings less than defined needs

—— earnings

---- needs

The earnings which this family would have required to reach the supplementary benefit scale plus 40 per cent and an average allowance for rent in 1972 is shown by the dashed line in the upper part of Fig. 5.1. As can be seen, the variation of need with age has much the same pattern as earnings but is rather more accentuated. As a result, earnings at the lowest decile are less than sufficient to meet the supplementary benefit plus forty per cent standard in earlier years; they are also insufficient as the man nears retirement when his earnings drop and his wife's earnings cease. The lower part of Fig. 5.1 provides an up-to-date version of the diagram used by Rowntree to illustrate the life-cycle of poverty. As found by him in 1899, income is likely to fall short of needs when there are dependent children and in old age. The period of 'comparative plenty' comes in the 40s and 50s, when there are no dependent children and both husband and wife are at work. Even in this period, however, the family's disposable income is only some £5 above its needs, so that the margin is not particularly generous. At this point, the low pay of women becomes of considerable importance for the family.

JOB SECURITY AND UNEMPLOYMENT

The picture of the career of the low paid worker described above gives an impression of security which he is unlikely to enjoy. He cannot look forward at the age of twenty-one to the certainty of earning even at the lowest decile. One indicator of this uncertainty is the make-up of pay for unskilled manual workers. Basic pay only constitutes 68 per cent of their earnings, compared with 91 per cent for non-manual workers. More important still is the fact that the low paid worker also faces a greater risk of losing his job. Fig. 5.1 assumed that he remained employed throughout his working life, but even on favourable assumptions about the overall state of the economy this seems highly unlikely. The Registrar General's figures for the male unemployment rate by socio-economic group gave the following results for 1966:

Unemployment rate per cent

Unskilled manual	6.8
Personal service workers	4.9
Semi-skilled manual	3.0
Agricultural workers	2.5
Skilled manual	1.8
Foremen, supervisors	1.3
Professional	0.8
Average	2.6

(Source: N. Bosanquet, 'Government and Unemployment 1966 – 1970' mimieograph).

The unemployment rate for unskilled manual workers was over two and a half times the average, and Bosanquet suggests that the gap may be even wider than these figures suggest.

Unemployment does not necessarily lead to poverty. A person drawing National Insurance earnings-related benefit can be confortably above the supplementary benefit level. The low paid worker, however, as a result of repeated or lengthy unemployment may well have exhausted his entitlement to the short-term supplement or indeed to the basic National Insurance benefit. He is much more likely to be among the large number who depend solely on supplementary benefits. (For discussion of the 'hierarchy' of benefits in unemployment, see A. Sinfield, 'Unemployment Compensation and Employment Security' mimeograph).

The association between low earnings and unemployment was brought out by the 1966 Circumstances of Families enquiry – see Table 5.3. For the sample as a whole, one in twenty five men had been unemployed in the preceding twelve months; for fathers whose earnings were insufficient to support their families at the national assistance level, the proportion was one in five. The enquiry also showed that absence through sickness was also much higher among low paid workers, a subject to which we now turn.

TABLE 5.3   *Absence From Work*

| | *Families where the father's earnings were* | |
| | *Above National Assistance Scale* | *Below National Assistance Scale* |
Absent because of		
Unemployment	4	21
Sickness	31	51
Other	5	7
All reasons	36	66

Source: *Circumstances of Families,* Table IV.18

SICKNESS ABSENCE AND ILL-HEALTH

The relationship between low pay and ill-health may be a general link between low living standards and sickness or may be a specific correlation between low paid jobs and occupation-related disease. Alternatively, the causality may run in the opposite direction. To distinguish between these explanations would require detailed epidemiological and other evidence, but for the present the important point is that sickness absence is a great deal higher for low paid workers. This was demonstrated not only the circumstances of families enquiry but also by the government study of sickness absence in 1961/2 – see Table 5.4.

The rate of sickness absence was considerably higher for unskilled workers than the average for all workers,* and this

*The rates of sickness absence may well be understated for Social Class I, since professional and managerial staff may not obtain a medical certificate, except for lengthy periods of sickness. It does not seem likely that this would have a large effect on the average for all workers.

difference was particularly marked at older ages. The length
of absence showed a similar pattern, with the number of days
being between two and three times as high for unskilled
workers as for social classes I and II.

TABLE 5.4   *Sickness Absence by Social Class and Age 1961-2*

Social Class	Age									
	25-34		35-44		45-54		55-59		60-63	
	Rate	Days	Rate	Days	Rate	Days	Rate	Days	Rate	Days
I and II Professional and Intermediate	172	2.9	154	3.4	159	4.4	198	7.4	230	11.1
III Skilled	259	5.3	254	6.6	276	9.1	324	14.0	364	20.4
IV Partly skilled	292	7.3	281	8.5	306	11.9	353	17.4	393	24.0
V Unskilled	330	9.9	338	12.7	356	15.8	402	22.7	422	27.3
All Classes	260	5.8	253	7.1	275	9.8	327	15.2	367	21.6

Notes: Rate = number of persons per 1000 who had one or more spells
       of incapacity for work.
       Days = days of incapacity per person

Source: Ministry of Pensions and National Insurance, *Report on an
Enquiry into the Incidence of Incapacity for Work,* Part II, HMSO, 1965
Table Aii.

The significance of sickness absence depends on the
financial resources to which the person has access. One
important source is the provision of sick pay by the employer. The 1970 earnings survey showed that 74 per cent
of all full-time adult male workers were covered by
schemes but that the proportion for unskilled manual
workers was rather lower (58 per cent). For workers in
the textile, clothing and footwear industries, the coverage
was as low as 26 per cent. Moreover, the benefits provided
varied considerably, with those for manual workers being
in many cases very much lower than for non-manual
workers. Incomes Data Services in a recent survey concluded that in the public sector 'non-manual workers
mostly have much longer periods of paid sick leave' and

in the private sector 'in the majority of the agreements we examined there are still more favourable provisions for white collar workers'. (Incomes Data Services, Studies No: 47 and 50 'Sick Pay', Parts 3 & 4, 1973). The Ministry of Labour report on sick pay schemes pointed out that 'normally, in the case of men manual workers, the "full wages" paid during sickness would be distinctly less than total earnings'. (Ministry of Labour, *Sick Pay Schemes*, p. 29). Low paid workers are, therefore, less likely both to be covered by a scheme and to receive full pay for the period of sickness. As a result they are dependent on National Insurance and supplementary benefit.

Sickness absence is only one way in which ill-health may affect the income of the low paid worker. It will also influence the kind of work he can choose and the intensity with which he can work. In the Circumstances of Families enquiry, 14 per cent of men with earnings below the national assistance scale said that their earnings were limited by ill-health, compared with 4 per cent of all families. Of the 52 wage-stopped families visited by the Supplementary Benefit Commission in its review of 1967, only a third said that they were in good health. (Administration of the Wage Stop, *HMSO*, 1967).

OLD AGE

It has been argued above that low paid workers are more likely to be out of employment and that they are less likely to have resources on which they can draw in these periods of need. Old age is different, in that everyone retires at some stage, but the inadequacy of resources to meet need at this stage of the low paid worker's life is just as important. In Fig. 5.1, the low paid worker was assumed to retire on a National Insurance pension of £10.90 (for a couple) but this is less than enough to raise him to the bare supplementary benefit level let alone forty per cent above. The supplementary benefit level (including the long term addition) comes to £11.25 a week before allowing for any housing costs, so that without any other source of income he will definitely fall below.

How likely is it that the low paid worker will be able to supplement his basic pension from other sources when he retires? The main additional source which he might have is an occupational pension; however, although private pension schemes now cover two-thirds of the male labour force, fewer low paid workers belong to such schemes. The 1970 New Earnings Survey showed that 78 per cent of non-manual male full-time workers belonged to pension schemes, whereas the corresponding proportion for manual workers was 50 per cent, and for unskilled manual workers 38 per cent. Similarly, in the earnings range £17-£20, in which the low paid worker would then have been, the proportion of manual workers covered was 36 per cent. Moreover, those low paid workers who do belong to an occupational scheme are likely to receive below-average benefits. The 1971 survey by the Government Actuary makes a number of comparisons between staff schemes and manual schemes, and on nearly all counts the latter are inferior. (Government Actuary, *Occupational Pension Schemes, 1971.* See also D. Wedderburn, 'Workplace Inequality', *New Society,* 9 April, 1970.) Over half of manual workers covered by schemes receive a pension calculated on a flat cash amount per year of service, which offers much less protection against inflation than the terminal salary schemes covering 85 per cent of staff members – see Table 5.5. Only 38 per cent of manual workers have an unconditional widow's pension on death after retirement, compared with 60 per cent of staff members. The effects of this discrimination between manual and non-manual workers were illustrated by the finding that in 1965 the average occupational pension drawn by manual workers was only one third of that of non-manual workers. The average amount received by manual workers was some 35 per cent of the National Insurance pension for a couple.

TABLE 5.5   *Staff and Manual Occupational Pension Schemes 1971, Public and Private Sector*

| | Proportion of members | |
	Staff	Manual
Pension Formula		
Terminal Salary	85	28
Flat accrual	2	59
Other	13	13
Ill-Health Pension		
More than accrued pension	46	22
Accrued pension	20	19
Less than accrued pension	28	54
Other	6	5
Widow's Pension *		
On death in service	62	55
On death after retirement (unconditional)	60	38

Note: * Male members only

Source: Government Actuary, *Occupational Pension Schemes 1971.* Tables 22, 32, 36 and 40.

It appears therefore that the low paid worker stands only a one in three chance of receiving an occupational pension, and even if this equalled the average for all manual workers it would increase his pension by less than £4. *Since the low paid worker is likely to do worse than average, it seems reasonable to conclude that very few are likely to be comfortably above the supplementary benefit level.

*Those not covered by an occupational scheme will receive a graduated pension, but the amounts involved are extremely small.

A second possible source of income in old age is saving in the form of either real assets, such as a house or consumer durables, or financial assets, such as money in the post office or savings bank. It should, however, have been clear from the analysis of the previous section that the margin for saving out of earnings was very small. The only period in which it would have been at all possible is that after the children had left home and, combined with poor investment opportunities, this means that savings can scarcely be expected to make any significant contribution to incomes in old age. In the same way, it is very unlikely that the low paid worker would have been able to buy his own house. Applying the $2\frac{3}{4}$ x earning's rule of the building societies to the man on £22 a week would mean that the most on which he could hope to get a mortgage would be a house costing £3,000 – if he could find one.

The low paid worker is likely therefore to end his days dependent on supplementary benefits. In this he will not be alone, since some 40 per cent of retirement pensioners have incomes below the supplementary benefit level, but he is likely to be among those most in need.

THE LESSONS TO BE DRAWN

The main aim of this paper has been to argue that low earnings are more important than an analysis of the immediate causes of poverty would suggest. Low pay must be seen more generally as a disadvantage in the labour market, and as associated with high incidence of job instability and ill-health and with the absence of fringe benefits. The low paid worker is more vulnerable to the interruption or loss of earning power, and lacks the resources to meet such needs. Low earnings mean that people cannot save for emergencies or for old age. They cannot get a mortgage and the only way in which they can borrow is through HP or not paying the electricity bill. In these and other ways, low pay plays an important role in the cycle of poverty.

This conclusion is significant since poverty is often viewed as something which could happen to anyone – either as a result of bad luck (losing one's job or becoming sick) or on account of the natural process of growing old. Related to this is the belief that much poverty is transitory, that is a temporary disruption or one associated with one particular stage of the life-cycle. This view, however, is highly misleading. People may not spend their entire lives in poverty, as Rowntree's diagram illustrates, but there are many forces making for the continuity of poverty and its recurrence with predictable frequency. As has been argued, low pay is a thread which runs throughout people's working lifetimes and beyond into retirement, and what may appear at first sight to be 'bad luck' is likely to be related to labour market disadvantage. Poverty does not happen to just anyone.

6. Low Pay and Fiscal Policy

Roy Moore
Research Officer with the Trade Union Research Unit

The object of this contribution is to look beyond the concept of low pay as indicated by gross money earnings,
and to consider the degree to which the low paid are
further adversely affected in terms of their real take-
home pay. All indications seem to point in the same
direction: that the initial disadvantage of the low paid
is aggravated by a vicious combination of relatively large
stoppages, high effective marginal tax rates, and rising
prices.

There are many diverse factors at work in this respect,
including income tax, national insurance contributions,
means-tested benefits, indirect taxation and differential
rates of price increase for different expenditure items.
The intention here is to consider each in turn, but in
doing so to build up an assessment of their cumulative
effect. It is not my intention to distract attention from
the causes of low pay, or from trade union efforts to
increase low wages, but rather to emphasise some wider
dimensions of low pay disadvantages.

DIRECT TAXES

It is generally assumed that progressiveness is a characteristic of both income tax and National Insurance contributions. The progressive principle of direct taxation
(i.e., that liability to tax should increase at least proportionately with income) is not always evident in practice.

As far as income tax is concerned, it can be shown that a 'tax hollow' exists for the range of earnings between twice and five times the national average, which implies that the low paid are within a less favoured category of tax liability relative to many of their higher-paid counterparts (N. Kaldor, *Evidence to Select Committee on Tax Credits*). Moreover, and more obviously, a low paid worker crossing the earnings threshold at which tax liability begins, faces a high jump in his marginal rate of tax from zero to thirty per cent, a jump far higher than any confronting the surtax payer.

The incidence of income tax is determined by the rate of tax charged and by the threshold earnings level at which tax is first payable, which in turn is governed by the scale of the main tax allowances. Two sets of tendencies have operated over recent years to ensure that the low paid face greater tax liability than a decade ago.

First, the reduced rates of taxation at lower income levels were abolished in the 1969 and 1970 Budgets. Second, the increases in money earnings which have occurred have brought more low paid workers above the tax threshold, although rising prices have meant that the real value of their higher earnings has not kept pace with the money increase. Tax thresholds have not been increased sufficiently to compensate for this tendency. This can be illustrated in several ways:

(1) In October 1964 the married couple with two children would begin to pay tax at £736 per year income. In April 1973 the threshold stands at £1,116 a year, but between these dates the Retail Price Index has increased from 107.9 to 176.7. The result is that this family pays tax now with an income level at October 1964 prices of £682 a year, or £54 less (£90 at today's prices). The 'real' tax threshold has fallen by over £1.50 a week.

(2) The tax threshold for a married man with two children has fallen from around national average earnings

119

just after the war (102.9 per cent in 1946-7) to little over half national average earnings (58.6 per cent) in 1971-2. (Michael Meacher: 'The Malaise of the Low Paid Worker' in *A Special Case*, ed. J. Hughes and R. Moore, Penguin, 1972, p. 93).

(3) On top of this, whereas the rates of tax on the first slices of income above the threshold were only 14 per cent and 23 per cent (allowing for earned income allowance) between 1965 and 1970, the low paid worker now faces the full 30 per cent standard rate immediately he crosses the threshold.

In summary, the combined effects of the abolition of lower tax rates together with inflation mean that more relatively lower paid workers pay more tax at higher rates than ever before. Whilst the tendency of 'fiscal drag' applies to all earnings levels in an inflationary economy, there is much evidence that the low paid have been the hardest hit. This is partly due to changes in tax thresholds and tax rates, and partly to the differential impact of inflation which, along with the harsh impact of cut-off points for entitlement to various benefits on the total effective marginal tax rate facing low paid workers, is considered below.

Whilst graduated contributions have, since 1961, introduced an earnings-related element into National Insurance employee contributions, the continued existence of – and increases in – the flat rate element, together with the cut-off point, qualify any progressiveness in their structure. Thus the annual article on 'Incidence of Taxes and Social Service Benefits in 1971' (*Economic Trends*, November 1972, p. xi) admits that... 'the present National Insurance contributions (particularly the flat rate contributions) are mildly regressive . . .' It can be shown from Table 1 (page xix) of the same article that National Insurance contributions account for around

5 per cent of household income for the low paid, but only 2 or 3 per cent of higher income. It has also shown how National Insurance contributions have increased as a percentage of average earnings over the post-war period, from 3.5 per cent in 1948 to 5.7 per cent in 1970. (F. Wilkinson and H. A. Turner, 'The Wage Tax Spiral and Labour Militancy' in *Do Trade Unions Cause Inflation?*, Jackson, Turner and Wilkinson, C.U.P., 1972, p. 63). These authors also confirm the regressiveness of contributions, which they estimate as 7.2 per cent of lowest decile manual earnings but only 4.4 per cent of the highest decile in 1970. (page 70).

The combined effect of income tax and national insurance deductions can thus be seen to militate against the low paid more sharply than against the average or high paid worker. It is also clear that this adverse effect is sharper today than a decade or more ago.

EXPENDITURE PATTERNS OF THE LOW PAID

There are two further ways in which the low paid suffer relatively more than others, in consequence of their expenditure patterns. First, greater proportions of their spending are claimed by indirect taxation; and second, they devote greater proportions of their incomes to goods whose prices have risen most steeply. Each of these is considered in turn. Official statistics have shown indirect taxes taken as a whole to be regressive, with relatively lower income households paying as great or greater percentages of their income into indirect taxation than higher income families. (Economic Trends, November 1972, Table F, p xi). These figures refer to the position in 1971, so it is fair to assume that the current position, following the introduction of value added tax, is even more regressive.

Whilst indirect taxes are by their very nature regressive, in that they tax a purchase at a standard rate without regard to the income-level of the purchaser, it was possible for a Chancellor of the Exchequer to organise the application of different rates of purchase tax in such a way that a rough element of progressiveness could be introduced. Thus, luxury and income-elastic items could be taxed at the higher rates of purchase tax, whilst essentials could carry lower or zero rates. V.A.T. is much less flexible in this respect, and the effect of its replacing purchase tax and selective employment tax can only be to introduce more regressiveness into the indirect tax structure. V.A.T. has increased the prices of regularly-purchased basic and essential goods, whilst reducing the price of less commonly purchased consumer durable and luxury items. The low paid inevitably suffer most under V.A.T.

It is not only indirect taxes which have an adverse effect on the low paid family's budget: their whole expenditure pattern is concentrated on those basic goods and services whose prices have increased most rapidly. The low paid devote greater proportions of their expenditure in particular to food, housing, and fuel. Between December 1970 and December 1972 the price index for food increased by 22.2 per cent, for housing by 24.2 per cent, and for fuel by 18.0 per cent, all higher than the overall increase in the Retail Price Index of 17.4 per cent. Meat, fish, fruit and vegetables all increased by between 30 and 40 per cent over the period.

The relevance of these figures is not simply that their impact was most harshly felt by the low paid, but also that they are all to some extent either government controlled, or under the direct influence of government policies. Government economic policies do not only operate fiscally through taxation, but also through subsidies, tariffs, price guarantees, money and credit, public expenditure programmes, and now too the EEC Common Agricultural Policy. It is largely the effect of government policies in these areas that is responsible for the disproportionate increases in price of those goods to which the low paid are obliged to devote disproportionate amounts of their income. It is difficult to assess on the basis of published data how great is disparity between the rising prices which face the low paid and the general rate of inflation as measured by the official Retail Price Index.

Our calculations in the Trade Union Research Unit suggest that the disparity is less than $1/2$ per cent per annum, although full price and expenditure details are not available, and nor are adequate data on housing (*Trade Union Research Unit's Technical Notes* on the Retail Price Index Nos 3, 7, 10, 13). Nevertheless, even if the discrepancy is small, it can become very significant in the context of increases in real take-home pay. For in periods when the average worker's real take-home pay (i.e., after allowing for deductions and the rise in the Retail Price Index) is rising at no more than 1 per cent per annum, as has often been the case, then the differential effect of price increases upon the low paid can be seen to cancel out a significant proportion of this increase.

ENTITLEMENT TO SOCIAL SERVICE BENEFITS.

The existence of many important means-tested social benefits with income-linked cut-off points means that the low paid worker can face an effective marginal tax rate far in excess of the 35 per cent take of income tax and national insurance contributions. The major means-tested benefits are family income supplement (FIS), free school meals, rent and rate rebates, and free medicines/dental and optical treatment, although there are over forty means-tested benefits altogether, such as school milk and uniforms. As earnings rise, entitlement to benefit is either reduced or removed altogether, according to income level and often also family size. The crucial range of incomes through which the various cut-off points operate is between £20 and £27 a week, so that it is the low paid worker who is really caught in the 'poverty trap', as it has come to be known (Frank Field and David Piachaud, 'The Poverty Trap', *New Statesman*, 3 December 1971). Although entitlement to FIS is now permitted to continue for a year irrespective of any pay rise following its initial payment, it is still quite possible for a low paid worker to face an effective marginal tax rate of over 100 per cent, and quite common for him to suffer an overall effective deduction of over 50 per cent of a pay rise.

Moreover, the number of low paid workers facing these penal marginal rates is very high when compared with the number on high incomes facing equivalent marginal surtax rates. Michael Meacher has shown that 330,000 low paid workers are subject to a 'poverty tax surcharge' of 50 per cent or more, whilst only 180,000 high income earners (£7,000 a year or more) face surtax rates higher than 50 per cent. (Michael Meacher, *Fairness and the Budget,* New Statesman, 2 March 1973).

It is important nevertheless to remember that the primary problem of poverty must not be subordinated to concentration on the poverty trap. This is particularly crucial since so many low paid workers fail to claim the benefits to which they are entitled, but which require familiarity, form-filling and a means-test before they can be claimed. The contrast between an owner-occupier, whose tax liability adjustment is automatically performed on his behalf by his building society and/or insurance company, and whose tax allowance tends to rise with income, and the tenant who can only obtain rent and rate rebates after a means test and a formal application, only to see their value reduced as his income increases, is a striking example of inequity and double standards which penalises the lower paid in yet another way.

The whole apparatus of means-tested benefits, ill-considered, badly co-ordinated and harshly applied, represents an incredible *Catch – 22* situation for the low paid worker. His failure to claim, or to submit to a means-test, prohibits him from receiving that to which he is formally entitled, and leaves him worse off than the state has provided he should be. But equally if he takes advantage of means-tested benefits, he incurs high effective marginal tax rates as his income increases. As a final irony the upward revisions made in cut-off points from time to time ensure that the poverty trap simply catches him up again after a brief period of non-entitlement. It is a case of poverty, the devil, or its trap, the deep blue sea.

OVERALL EFFECTS ON REAL TAKE-HOME PAY.

The extent to which the low paid worker has been able to raise his gross pay is difficult to determine. The tendency of earnings data to 'regress towards the mean' over-time, and the difference in results obtained over different time periods both tend to cloud the issue. It appears that lower paid workers have secured bigger percentage increases than others of late (*New Earnings Survey,* 1968, 1970, 1971 and 1972, Department of Employment), but on the other hand there is no evidence of any significant change over time in the lowest decile and lower quartile earnings expressed as percentages of the median.

Nevertheless, calculations of the differential effects of income tax, national insurance contributions and inflation as measured by the Retail Price Index seem to confirm that whichever gross pay figures are used, the pay gaps are widened when we move from gross money earnings to real take-home pay (Turner et al. in *Do Trade*

Unions Cause Inflation? pages 77–78 and 89–94, C.U.P.
1972). If we superimpose on top of such calculations the
added disadvantages to the low paid of the differential
impact of price increases upon their particular spending
patterns, the unfavourable incidence of direct taxation,
and the swelling of their effective marginal tax rates by
means-tested benefits, then the real face of the problem of
low pay stands out starkly. A whole set of obstacles is operating to prevent the real value of the low paid worker's
take-home pay from rising.

But to see the degree of discrimination operating
against the low paid worker in the full perspective we
need to look at trends in the taxation liabilities of higher
incomes and of companies over the same period. Over
the period from 1960 – 70, the average tax rate at £600
real earned income rose 40 per cent; at £20,000 the rise
was only 4 per cent. (Turner et al. p.79). The percentage
of income taken as taxation from corporate profits fell
from 36·5 per cent in 1949 – 52, to 19·0 per cent in
1965 – 68; whilst in the same period the tax-take from
wages and salaries rose from 9·8 per cent to 15·5 per cent.
(Turner et al. p.80).

The imbalance has become still more acute during the
Heath Government, with two reductions in the rate of
corporation tax, and budgets particularly favourable to
higher incomes, whether earned or unearned. The effects
of the 1971 budget, particularly the extension of earned
income allowance without limit, provided massive increases in post-tax income for higher income groups. The
married man on £25,000 a year, for instance, would gain
some £2,800 a year in take-home pay – an increase of
35 per cent. The position of unearned income remaining
after tax has similarly been increased by Budget changes,
with the effect that a man on £20,000 a year investment
income is left with £1,704 more now than previously –
an increase of 31 per cent on post-tax income.

Finally, this year's Budget has reduced tax liability – largely for high-earners – by some £300m. a year in moving to the unified tax structure. The £20,000 a year married man gains £516 a year in take-home pay, which, it will be noted, is over twice the maximum *gross* pay increase permitted to any individual under Phase Two.

The combined effect of the tax changes on unearned income suggests that the £20,000 a year married man has increased his take-home pay in real terms by 15 per cent between 1970/71 and 1973/74, whilst the real increase for the £1,500 a year man is less than 2 per cent. All the evidence, from this contribution, from the Trade Union Research Unit, and from elsewhere, is that the low paid worker has almost certainly done even less well in terms of increasing his real take-home pay. (see *Trade Research Units Occasional Papers,* Effects of the 1971 Budget on Company Directors' Take Home Pay (1972) Income Increases Under Phase II (1973) and Changes in Income Tax 1970/1 – 1973/4 (1973)).

CONCLUSIONS.

This contribution has attempted to identify focal points for policy changes and fiscal measures. Its analysis contains implicit indications for remedies, together with considerations which support the strength of the low paid worker's collective bargaining case. The following points seem to be of sufficient importance to list in this final section.

(1) In some cases the low paid worker may have been hit as an unintended consequence of an otherwise motivated Chancellor's measure. If the intention is to take workers out of the tax paying bracket, or to simplify the tax system and structure, then this must not be permitted to act against the interests of the low paid. Moreover,

127

it must be followed up as and when necessary, by consequent adjustment in following years. This is particularly true with regard to the raising of the tax threshold, which ought to be regularly and automatically increased in response to rates of inflation.

(2) There is strong evidence that our income tax structure is not progressive over a significant range of income, and that the successive budgets of this Government have served only to extend and deepen this degree of inequity. There is also a strong element of regressiveness in the scale of National Insurance contributions.

(3) The extent to which low paid workers are hit by fiscal policies is not confined to direct taxation, and again there are strong reasons to presume that the introduction of V.A.T. is aggravating the degree of regressiveness.

(4) The effect of indirect taxation and other government economic policies and measures upon prices has a particularly adverse effect on low paid workers, due to their expenditure patterns. The Government's claim that many of these price increases are outside its control is blatantly false. To some extent workers can be protected against rising prices through threshold clauses, but equally the government need not accept the inevitability of either the pace or the incidence of retail price increases.

(5) Universal flat-rate benefits are the only equitable form of social service provision, and is immensely preferable to means-tested benefits. The proposals for tax credits are worthy of consideration only either if they are applied as quickly as possible (e.g., universal child credits now), or if their levels are increased sufficiently to compensate for inflation.

(6) The acceptability of the provision of the government's counter-inflation policy cannot be acceptable as long as they oblige workers to accept increases less than are required to permit take-home pay to rise sufficiently to cover prices. Moreover, they can only be fairly judged

against the fiscal background of budgets highly favourable to the take-home pay of the higher paid.

(7) Finally, both the coverage and timeliness of official statistics could be improved to permit a true view of the movement in real take-home pay at different income levels. The Retail Price Index is too general to be applicable to lower income families; the sources of data are too diverse to permit adequate calculations of take-home pay; there is no index of real take-home pay available for any income group, let alone the low paid worker; the *Economic Trends* articles on Incidence of Taxation and Benefits appear too late to be applicable to contemporary circumstances; and the Wage Rate Indices of the Department of Employment are misleading and practically meaningless. In the absence of adequate data, it is difficult enough even to assess the dimensions and the nature of the low pay problem, and represents an additional obstacle in the way of reconnecting policy changes.

7. Low Pay and Social Policy

Frank Field
Director of the Child Poverty Action Group

To be low paid is, for many, similar to having a wasting disease; after a time it affects not only the whole of one's own life but one's family's life too. Professor Atkinson has shown in his contribution how the low paid worker is likely to suffer greater job insecurity, a higher sickness rate and carry his poverty into retirement. This paper looks at the repurcussions of low pay on our system of social security, and how its existence adversely affects a large number of families even after the bread-winner is unable to work. The paper looks at the extent to which the incentive to work is retained even for jobs paying poverty wages, and how large numbers of claimants are denied benefit in order to make them available for low paying employment. In doing so, the first part examines the wage-stop rule and the second discusses the four-week or work-shy rule.

THE WAGE STOP

Under the Ministry of Social Security Act (1966) the Supplementary Benefits Commission (SBC), the body responsible for administering supplementary benefits, is forbidden to pay men more in benefit than the rewards they would receive while in work. The Act states that, unless there are exceptional circumstances,

130

'The weekly amount of any supplementary allowance payable to that person shall not exceed what would be his net weekly earnings if he were engaged in full-time work in his normal occupation.'

So, despite popular belief, low paid workers are not allowed to move out of work to draw more in benefit, and Table 7.1 shows the number of men who were prevented from doing just this in each year since 1967.

TABLE 7.1   Number of Supplementary Benefit recipients with a wage-stop deduction each year since 1967

Year	Number	Amount of weekly wage stop deduction £
1967	37,550	1.68
1968	32,410	1.12
1969	34,040	1.64
1970	35,620	1.95
1971	23,180	1.47

Source: Annual Special Sample Inquiries (DHSS)

The Department of Health and Social Security (DHSS) justifies the wage-stop in the following terms. As supplementary benefit

'cannot be paid to bring the income of a man in full-time employment up to supplementary benefit levels, the statutory provisions recognize that it would be wrong in equity to bring the income of a man of low earning capacity up to these levels because he happened to be unemployed or temporarily sick when there was nothing which could be done for his counterpart in full-time work' (Administration of the Wage-Stop, HMSO, 1967, p.2).

And the SBC adds:

'The wage-stop is not, therefore, a cause of family poverty; it is a harsh reflection of the fact that there are many men in work living on incomes below the supplementary benefit standard' (p.2).

While the second part of the sentence is true, the first is based on rather doubtful reasoning. The wage-stop ruling is certainly a cause of harsh poverty for some unemployed men and their families. That these families fare little better when in work must be their only consoling thought as each week they draw a benefit which is deliberately set at a level below the official poverty line.

HOW THE WAGE STOP WORKS

The Commission believes it has 'a clear duty to see that it is administered in as fair and as understanding a way as possible.' How does this work out in practice?

Although at first sight the wage-stop might appear a simple rule to apply, experience proves the opposite. In many instances the Commission claims it is impossible to know with any certainty what a man's previous earnings were. Likewise, how do you judge what his potential earnings are after he has been out of work for six months or more?

The Commission, partly for administrative convenience, but also because it wishes to treat supposedly similarly placed claimants in an identical manner throughout the country, uses the local authority labourer and light labourer rates (these are the lowest nationally negotiated rates). At the end of six months labourers are wage-stopped at the local authority wage rates regardless of past earnings, and at the end of twelve months the Commission discounts any craft skills a wage-stopped claimant may have. This procedure, which arbitrarily forces the income of many families below the poverty line, is not based on law but is an example of the way the SBC exercises part of its considerable battery of discretionary powers against the claimant's best interest.

In 1971 nearly two-thirds of all wage-stopped men had their benefit limited to the labourer or light labourer wage level. The study by Ruth Lister (*The Administration of the Wage Stop,* CPAG, 1972) – who kindly commented on this paper, as did Tony Atkinson – cites a number of examples she came across in her research where men were clearly entitled to full benefit but were nevertheless wage-stopped. Although wage-stopped families are supposed to receive a notice of assessment (which is something like a wage slip) setting out how their benefit is calculated, it appears that few do. As only the exceptional claimant knows about his correct entitlement, and almost none have heard of the wage-stop, let alone of it applying to them, few claimants appeal against the decision.

The Act expressly states that the wage-stop should not apply if there are 'exceptional circumstances' but the Commission not only fails to tell most families they are wage-stopped, but has not yet got around to divulging what constitutes 'exceptional circumstances'. This is an example of the *Catch 22* situation which surrounds the exercise of discretion. The Commission claims that it can only say if there are exceptional circumstances if an individual family is cited. Only then does it become possible to take all the relevant circumstances into account and decide whether there are exceptional circumstances. This argument is used to justify the refusal to publish the criteria for deciding whether there are exceptional circumstances. But presumably such criteria do exist, for otherwise the officers might treat differently similarly placed claimants, although the yardstick would appear to be pretty severe. Ruth Lister cites a case where a family with nine children had £9.60 to live on after their rent had been paid. One would have thought that the existence of nine children alone constituted 'exceptional circumstances'. It did under the much hated Unemployment Assistance Board (see Tony Lynes *Guide to Supplementary Benefits,* Penguin, 1972, p. 121) but not, seemingly, with the SBC.

The wage-stop rule can also apply to claimants who are drawing benefit because they are sick, but in these cases it is discretionary and the SBC policy is to apply it where it is believed that their illness will last less than thirteen weeks. Only exceptionally do doctors state that an illness will incapacitate a claimant for more than three months. As a result, most claimants who were previously drawing low wages and who became ill are automatically wage-stopped. The ruling should be lifted after three months – but it appears that the Commission makes no check on claimants whose illness continues beyond the thirteen weeks (and the thirteen week cut-off point is again for the SBC administrative convenience). Many families whose breadwinners are wage-stopped because at first sight theirs appeared a short-term illness, suffer the imposition of the wage-stop beyond this period.

Since April 1971 wage-stopped families have been awarded notional Family Income Supplement (FIS) payments. This new benefit was introduced in order to raise the incomes of family men earning very low wages to the poverty line. The measure therefore applied to wage-stopped families for, had they been in work, FIS would have been added to their take-home pay.

The effect of FIS on the number of wage-stopped families and the severity with which the rule is applied can be seen from Table One. Despite this measure, the aim of which is to raise families to at least the supplementary benefit level, over 23,000 families remain wage-stopped (and over 50,000 family men in work earn less than their theoretical SB entitlement). But the size of the wage-stop deduction has been reduced. On average, wage-stopped families have their benefit reduced to £1·47 below the supplementary benefit poverty line. As with all averages it tells us nothing about the dispersion around the average. Table 7.2 sets out the range of wage-stop deductions in 1971. Although over 2,600 families suffer a deduction from their supplementary benefit of 25p or less a week, 340 families are forced to live at least £5 a week below the official poverty line.

TABLE 7.2   Size of Wage Stop deduction 1971

Size of wage-stop	Number of families affected
25p and less	2,639
26p – 50	2,683
51p – 75	3,019
76p – £1	2,173
£1.01 – £1.50	3,780
£1.51 – £2	2,979
£2.01 – £2.50	1,869
£2.51 – £3	1,408
£3.01 – £4	1,576
£4.01 – £5	722
£5.01 and over	340
Total 23,180	Total 23,180

Source: DHSS one in forty sample.

Because families are forced to live below the poverty line, it is not surprising that they find it difficult to manage. Indeed, one DHSS official has gone on record as saying that if wage-stopped families do manage to make ends meet, then it may be because the family is in receipt of some undisclosed earnings. Such a statement probably says more about the person uttering it than about the honesty of families on benefit. However, the Commission is aware of the difficulties families face living on a very low level of income and officers are supposed to visit wage-stopped families at least once every thirteen weeks. It is clear from the 'A' Code (one of the Department's rule books which is classified under The Official Secrets Act) that some onus is put on the visiting officers during these visits to find out whether additional help is needed. The 'A' Code instructs them to look out for evidence of serious difficulties such as undernourished children, sub-

stantial rent arrears, pressing debts and serious defi-
ciencies in clothing and bedding. It is amazing that the
Department should be asked to operate a rule which
might result in any one of these repercussions; but where
there are signs of hardship the officers are supposed to
award single lump sum payments rather than make a
regular weekly addition to the family's benefit or, as it
is called, 'adding back'. The 'A' Code makes it clear that
lump sum awards are preferred as regular weekly additions
may create a disincentive to return to work.

It is these throw-away comments, tucked away in
secret codes, which tell us one, if not the, reason for the
wage-stop ruling; to get men back into work, and if need
be into jobs paying very low wages. A similar admission
was made by the present Secretary of State for Social
Services during a conversation with the author. The
meeting took place shortly after the introduction of FIS,
and the Minister was claiming, quite rightly, that the
number of wage-stop claimants had been reduced considerably. The Minister was asked: 'If the wage-stop now
applies to so few, why not abolish the rule altogether?'
His immediate reply was the need to retain an incentive
for men to return to work. This statement did not go
unchallenged; his senior civil servants were quick to
point out that the official view was to maintain equality
with low wage earners and not to preserve a work incentive.

GRADUATED BENEFITS

The wage-stop principle is not confined to supplementary
benefits. Since the introduction of graduated contributory
benefits in 1966, a wage stop is also applied to claimants
who would otherwise draw more than 85 per cent of their
normal earnings from sickness or unemployment benefit.
So although low wage earners have no option but to contribute to the graduated insurance scheme, they are

refused full benefit if this is valued at more than 85 per cent of their earnings.

The Department has been able to supply data on the number of sick and unemployed wage-stop claimants drawing graduated benefit for May 1971. 1.2 per cent of sick and 0.4 per cent of unemployed beneficiaries were disallowed the full benefit. In actual numbers this meant that 19,200 sick and 5,760 unemployed claimants drew less than their full entitlement. If the same proportion of claimants had the wage-stop applied against them at other times of the year, the numbers so affected would grow considerably. For example, it would have meant that 60,480 claimants for graduated sickness benefit were wage-stopped in December 1971.

THE WORKSHY RULES

The four-week rule, as it is known, is an even clearer demonstration of the way social policy is made to take account of the needs of a low wage economy. With the widespread existence of low wages there is a danger that adequate social security benefits will undermine the will to work. The wage-stop prevents people being better off out of work than following their normal occupation, and the four-week rule 'helps' people to choose employment, even if the work pays poverty wages.

The rule was announced by Judith Hart, the Minister for Social Security, on 25 July 1968. In a Parliamentary Answer, the Minister informed the House that:

'When people first claim, most fit, young, single persons will be told, whenever work is available in the locality, that they should be able to find work within four weeks and that after four weeks a supplementary allowance will not be paid to them... (although) there will be every safeguard in the mass of genuine claimants. For example, if a supplementary allowance is refused or terminated, there is of course the right of

137

appeal to the independent local Supplementary Benefit Appeal Tribunal' (House of Commons, *Hansard,* 25 July 1968, vol 787, cols 213 and 214).

The number of claimants who have so far been penalized under the four-week rule totals over a quarter of a million (information from the DHSS). Not one penny has been spent on following up even a single claimant to see if, once what is often his only source of income is withdrawn, he finds employment. Claimants do not have to be offered a job, and refuse it, before benefit is denied. If the Department 'feels' (their language) jobs are available, then the four-week rule will apply in that locality.

When the rule was first introduced, the Minister claimed that it was in response to the 'strong (Labour) Party resentment about abuse' (*New Statesman,* 29 January 1971). A 'trial run' had taken place in a couple of South London offices and the response 'was encouraging . In one office, a single member of staff was assigned the duty of interviewing the long-term unemployed, and 'out of eighty (unemployed men) "on the list" half had been successfully encouraged into jobs, and had stayed in work. The other half were judged to be mentally disturbed, physically limited or psychologically maladjusted. Mrs Hart went on to say that there was not the staff to operate a similar control procedure in all offices ' ... with serious understaffing, an annual turnover of anything up to a third of the staff, and shocking premises, this was to dream dreams. Instead a blanket four-week rule would operate on all single, fit, unskilled men in areas where the Department of Employment believed jobs were available.'

Inevitably the rule has been arbitrarily applied. It has been operated in areas with over 5 per cent unemployment. And can a counter clerk, often so poorly paid that he is drawing FIS, tell if a man is fit? The evidence suggests he cannot. The author's own experience of taking one four-week rule case through from when the rule was first applied to a phone call from the Chairman of the Supplementary Benefits Commission asking for the name of the claimant so that it could be lifted, has been recalled elsewhere. ('Benefit Shy', *The Guardian*, 17 November 1971).

Not surprisingly, the claimant, who had been mentally ill, looked quite normal. The last thing he was going to do was advertize his illness. But, more important, no official had asked him if he had ever been mentally ill; the local appeal tribunal did not believe this to be a question to pose, and yet the 'AX' Code (yet another secret document classified under The Official Secrets Act), clearly states that the rule should never be applied against those who have been at any time mentally ill.

The experience of this one claimant is far from unique. In a preliminary report of a national survey of men against whom the four-week rule had been applied, Michael Meacher cites other examples of men who were far from fit but who had been categorized as work shy ('The ruled-out class,' *The Guardian*, 23 February, 1973). He was also able to report on what these 100 men did once they had been denied benefit. Some had taken any job, however inappropriate to their experience or skills. For example, a twenty four year old with two GCE 'A' levels felt forced to take a general labouring job. But even this kind of 'opportunity' was denied to some. One in six admitted stealing in order to make ends meet. Others lived by betting, male prostitution or by 'moving in' with a female in full-time work. A rather disappointing response for those who believed the four-week rule would strengthen the work ethic and other traditional values.

The introductory remarks to this paper openly stated that the author was putting forward a hypothesis that the four-week rule, if not exclusively designed to ensure that men were expelled from the welfare rolls in order to avail themselves of low paid jobs, certainly achieves this goal. How else can one explain what has already been written about the operation and the consequences of the rule? And how can one explain away the following information? Asked last year by Ralph Howell, a Norfolk MP, on how many men and women were registered for work but drew neither unemployment nor supplementary benefit, the Junior Minister at the Department of Employment replied there were about 144,000 males and 47,000 females, or: 'Twenty-one per cent of all registrants were receiving neither unemployment benefit nor supplementary benefit.' (House of Commons, *Hansard*, March 17 1972, vol 837, col 190.) Can a total of nearly 200,000 be accounted for by bank managers and similar people who have been retired early and have registered for work (but with not too much enthusiasm about gaining new employment) in order to be credited with their National Insurance contributions and so preserve their right to a full old age pension?

Of course, no Minister has gone on record and openly expressed the view that where the welfare state's values conflict with the needs of the market economy those values have to take second place. However, some have come pretty close to it. Take, for example, a statement by Judith Hart from her *New Statesman* letter: 'I must admit that I felt no sense of enormous guilt about encouraging the healthy to work.'

The Minister's apparent lack of shame was not fully shared by Sir Henry Fisher and his colleagues who criticized the practice of denying benefit before the claimant was offered a specific job. Sir Henry also defined what a suitable job should be in the following terms:

'We accept that a job should not be regarded as suitable if the net take-home pay (plus family income supplement if applicable) is less than the weekly sum which the person will receive if he remains on supplementary benefit. (see Report of the Committee on Abuse of Social Security Benefits, HMSO, 1973, pp 100 and 226).

CONCLUSION

While we are debating strategies against low pay, consideration should be given to the role the social security system should play in this. I would argue that instead of its values always being subordinated to those of the free market, it could, in the two areas discussed in this paper, challenge the market dominance. What would be the consequence of abolishing the wage-stop? In other words, of saying that workers should be free to opt out and draw benefit until such time as they are offered jobs paying above the state poverty line? And wouldn't the prospect of a decent level of reward be enhanced if no man was denied benefit until a suitable job was available – i.e., one which paid above benefit level? It would be interesting to find out.